THE
GREEN SMOOTHIE MIRACLE

Your Way to Increased Energy, Weight Loss, and Happiness

Erica Palmcrantz Aziz

photography by
Anna Hult

translated by Malou Fickling

Skyhorse Publishing

Skyhorse Publishing books may be purchased in bulk at special discounts for sales promotion, corporate gifts, fund-raising, or educational purposes. Special editions can also be created to specifications. For details, contact the Special Sales Department, Skyhorse Publishing, 307 West 36th Street, 11th Floor, New York, NY 10018 or info@skyhorsepublishing.com.

Skyhorse® and Skyhorse Publishing® are registered trademarks of Skyhorse Publishing, Inc.®, a Delaware corporation.

Visit our website at www.skyhorsepublishing.com.

10 9 8 7 6 5 4 3 2 1

2014 edition printed for Barnes & Noble, Inc.
ISBN: 978-1-4351-5512-1

Library of Congress Cataloging-in-Publication Data

Palmcrantz Aziz, Erica, 1977-
   The green smoothie miracle : your way to increased energy, weight loss, and happiness / Erica Palmcrantz Aziz ; photography by Anna Hult.
       pages cm
   Includes index.
   Summary: "Provides information about the health benefits of chlorophyll as well as smoothie recipes that incorporate a wide variety of fruits and vegetables"-- Provided by publisher.
   ISBN 978-1-62087-061-7 (hardcover : alk. paper)
   1. Vegetable juices--Therapeutic use. 2. Smoothies (Beverages)--Therapeutic use. 3. Reducing diets. I. Title.
   RM236.P34 2012
   613.2--dc23
                                   2012033098

Printed in China

The recipes, advice, and tips in this book are not intended as medical advice. Always consult a doctor before starting a new diet or wellness program.

To our magical Earth

Contents

Foreword

On being timely.

The little airport was dark, with not a cab in sight, as I raced up to the Arrivals just before midnight. I was late. A dark figure moved into the streetlight, visibly relieved. Erica!

My niece, whom I hadn't seen in at least ten years, apologized for getting the times mixed up—half past and half hours can be tricky when your mother tongue is not English. No matter, she was here at last!

The little girl I remembered as a chubby, giggling bundle of joy, with a complexion like pink marzipan that earned her the nick name of Miss Piggy, was now a young woman. There was so much to catch up on.

After a couple of weeks, yakking away in a mixture of English and Swedish, we traveled down the beautiful west coast to visit my daughter and her family. During the bumpy train ride I had discovered that Erica had a bad back, the painful result of an accident in her youth. She was in bad shape when we finally arrived at Jinjee's mountain home. No coffee and toast for breakfast, no burgers, no fries; just heaps of fruit, nuts, and veggies.

To suddenly change time zones and language can be tricky for anyone, but throw in a total change in diet and it boggles not only the mind, but the whole body. Anyway, it wasn't long after I had returned home that I got glowing reports on Erica's progress. She was pain-free and felt great, reveling in her new found energy and joy.

Seeing these two cousins today, I am reminded of how timely they are. In a world groaning under the weight of seven billion people, where many are suffering from famine and others from malnutrition due to poor food quality; where vast tracts of valuable land is used for cattle feed, instead of crops which benefit humans directly; where huge amounts of firewood, coal, and kilowatt hours are used to roast, bake, and boil food until it is unrecognizable; where stress and disease are rampant, then it makes so much sense to make changes for the better. We can not always change the world, or even our own families, but we can change our own lives in ways that may have beneficial repercussions in the world around us.

Thank you, Erica and Jinjee, for being just in time!

Christel Palmcrantz Garrick
Nanaimo, Vancouver Island , Canada

GREEN Smoothie Miracle

Introduction

It was a gray, foggy, and chilly November day, and I was feeling just like the weather. For some time, I had missed that spark of happiness in my life; I felt as though I were stuck on a treadmill. If this is the meaning of life I thought, I might as well quit altogether. Despite my kind partner and a good job with great colleagues and a good salary, I had a strong sense that there was more to life than this. I needed to create space for myself in order to think and invite something new into my life. And so, without knowing what I would do next, I decided to quit my job. My friends thought I was going a little crazy, but I felt I had no other choice; I had to get some distance from my everyday life. I just needed to get away.

Around that time, my cousin James told me that I should look at his sister Jinjee's new website, www.thegardendiet.com. James said that she ran a business from home while home schooling her four children, and that she probably could use some help. The next day, I visited the website and was greeted by images of wonderful fruits and vegetables, people glowing with energy and life, and pictures of my cousin Jinjee and her four children. However, at that moment I wasn't particularly impressed by the food or the message of the website.

My cousin Jinjee had always lived abroad, so I had met her on only a few occasions when she visited Sweden. I remembered her as extremely beautiful and charismatic. My family often spoke about how she and her husband lived in California, and how they ate oranges—lots of oranges! They also ate 100 percent raw, locally grown, and organic food.

Mustering up the courage, I nervously phoned the other side of the world and asked Jinjee if I could come over and help her with the children. She immediately said yes, though her husband, Storm, wondered if she had gone crazy!, Even though Jinjee and Storm lived in a little village in the mountains at that time, where there was not much happening, Storm was very nervous that Jinjee's blonde Swedish cousin was going to hang out in Los Angeles and certain that my father would call and yell at them if they didn't protect me. But Jinjee said, "She is family, of course she's welcome."

It wasn't until I was on the flight to America that I really started thinking about what I had gotten myself into. I didn't think much about food. At the time, I lived on a healthier version of a standard diet, and I assumed that there would certainly be some places in California where I could get regular food. My attitude was that fruits and vegetables are good, but not all the time.

When I arrived to their home with my aunt Christel in California, I was expecting to be greeted by pale, scrawny, people, because that's what you look like, I believed, when you eat only fruits, vegetables, nuts, and seeds. Instead, I saw that the whole Talifero family was glowing and healthy. Their cupboards were indeed filled with nuts, seeds, and dried fruit, and there were ninety pounds of oranges, avocados, and ripe peaches that had been picked that morning lying on the kitchen counter. There was also a young coconut in the fridge and some frozen bananas in the freezer. A little different than what I was used to.

I stayed with my cousins for ten weeks, and from the day I arrived, I ate 100 percent raw. I felt my spark for life coming back after just one week. My blood sugar imbalance stabilized, I lost a few pounds, and my upset stomach became calm. To me, stomach and mind go together. If my stomach is calm, I am also calmer and happier.

I read every raw food book in the house, and I completely embraced what I learned. Everything I read felt so right. This, I thought, is what my body has been longing for.

I am tremendously grateful to Storm and Jinjee for opening their home and arms to me, and for sharing their life experiences with me. Storm has eaten raw food for forty years, Jinjee for eighteen years, and their children have eaten 100 percent raw food since they were born. My cousins taught me everything they knew about the raw lifestyle. They have brought much joy to me and the world, and they will forever be my role models.

When I returned to Sweden, I became utterly confused. At that time, I could find only one raw food blog, which was inactive, and two living food institutes in Sweden, and I felt terribly alone. I didn't know what to eat, because the food wasn't of the same quality as it was in California, and organic food was hard to find. So, I started to experiment with the food I could find in Sweden and began to create my own recipes.

I wanted to share my encounter with raw food and demonstrate how easy it is to live raw. This resulted in my first book, *Raw food—A Complete Guide for Every Meal of the Day,* written with health journalist Irmela Lilja. It is a beginner's guide with easy and tasty recipes for anyone who wants to incorporate raw food into his or her life. The book became so popular that we decided to write a second book, *Raw Desserts*, which is all about making desserts the raw food way. Goodies are a great and easy way to include raw in your regular diet. The same goes for green smoothies, which I share with you in this book. They are quick and simple to make, taste fantastic, and at the same time, make the body very happy and provide it with plenty of nutrition.

In the book, you will meet Malin, Andreas, Filippa, and Dagger, who all have a connection to green smoothies. They will share their best recipes and tips and explain how they started with green smoothies. Read on for inspiration!

How I eat my green smoothies

Breakfast: I make either a green breakfast or a big batch of green smoothie and save whatever is left over in a bottle so that I can quickly boost my energy whenever I want to.

Snack: I drink whatever is left over from breakfast, or I have a sauerkraut juice—a healthy drink that contains plenty of fresh and healthy lactic acid bacteria. See the recipe for sauerkraut juice on page 155. If you prefer, you can buy it from your local health food store.

Lunch: I follow the axiom that you should eat like a prince for breakfast, a king for lunch, and a poor man for dinner; this helps ensure that you'll have energy throughout the day and that your digestive system performs optimally. (Read more about the digestive system on page 38.) This is why I usually make a more filling smoothie with avocado for lunch.

Snack: To prevent sugar cravings and tiredness that can creep up on you in the middle of the day, I like to have a sweet fruit or even go all out and have a green smoothie milkshake in the afternoon.

Dinner: When I don't feel like cooking dinner in the evening, I drink my green smoothie without the fruit, because fruit contains fruit sugar and additional carbohydrates.

Long Live Life!

About the Author

"To eat raw food is to celebrate and give yourself and
the earth the very best."

—Erica Palmcrantz Aziz

Erica Palmcrantz Aziz has been high raw vegan for over seven years. This means that her diet consists of at least 85 percent raw food. In Sweden, Erica is a well-established advocate of raw food and inspires people to find their way to eating raw food. She has written three books on the subject and has released a DVD.

Name: Erica Palmcrantz Aziz. **Age:** 35. **Lives:** Gothenburg, Sweden. **Family:** Husband Sam Aziz, 41 years, and daughter Saga, 5 years. **Does:** Inspires, writes books, and educates about raw food.

Why I like green smoothies:
"They take two minutes to make and give me a nice feeling of fullness and positive energy."

My favorite recipe:
"Spinach, cucumber, lime, ginger, and avocado with a tulsi tea base."

My best advice on how to start:
"Don't think—just make your smoothie. Try it four times before you decide if you like it or not. To enhance the flavor, add some extra fruit."

The funniest comment I got when I talked about green smoothies: "But we're not monkeys, are we?"

I drink my smoothies: "When don't I drink my green smoothies?!"

Love &
Gratitude

Love &
Gratitude

The Green Smoothie Miracle

More and more people are looking for ways to include raw food in their lives, but to different extents. People prefer food that's easy to make, simple, and tasty, and this is exactly the description of green smoothies. Everyone, regardless of how much raw food they choose to eat, can make green smoothies. They are quick, filling, and taste good. In addition, they give you more energy and make you slimmer and happier! This book gives you the answers to **Why, What, How, When, Where** to make delicious green smoothies, and it will teach you all about the nutritional goodness they contain. You will also find many tasty, mouthwatering recipes that will give you energy in under five minutes.

I want the recipes in the book to be a basis for your own creativity. Gradually let your feelings guide you to what you put into your green smoothies—we are unique beings, and it's important to take who you are into consideration. What makes you feel good? What are you in the mood for? What does your life look like at that particular moment?

Remember to prepare the drink with love, gratitude, and joy. Love and enjoyment also provide you with nutrition that you need, so if you find yourself sulking over a green smoothie, don't force it. Allow yourself to feel what food you're really craving, and then give yourself permission to eat it with the same gratitude and love as you would the green drink. You'll find that the desire to eat green will come back without any effort. It might take a while for your body to adjust to a new diet, but the body knows that the green leaves will give it a nutritional boost, and after a while, you will feel your body craving the green smoothies again.

There are many fantastic books on green smoothies, with plenty of interesting information. I want this book to be about the raw food lifestyle, with inspiring and beautiful images that awaken your desire and willingness to invite more green into your life. Follow me on a green trip to your natural weight, increased energy, and happiness!

Green is the new coffee—you gotta have it every day.

Increased Energy

Why Green Smoothies Give You Increased Energy

1   Green leaves make your body more alkaline (read more about this on page 27). Acidification of the body is unfortunately a result of the standard modern diet. Eating a diet containing alkaline is necessary in order for the body to feel as good as possible.

2   Your digestive system gets more rest than it would by eating a salad or regular food because the blender grinds the food. Digestion uses the most amount of energy of all the processes in the body, so when we facilitate digestion, we leave the body with more energy for other things.

3   You devour large amounts of green leaves that are incredibly high in the essential minerals your body needs to function.

4   You devour lots of live enzymes (read more about this on page 14). Live enzymes are proteins that act as a catalyst. Your cells need live enzymes to repair themselves and to build new, healthy cells. Live enzymes make you shine!

5   Green smoothies increase hydrochloric acid in your stomach, which is essential for both the digestion and absorption of food.

6   Chlorophyll is the green color of the leaves—in short, chlorophyll is encapsulated sunlight. Chlorophyll is similar to the chemical composition of our blood. The more chlorophyll-rich foods you eat, the easier it is for your blood and your internal organs to clean themselves. And the cleaner your blood is, the less your internal organs will be burdened, which means you have a lower risk of getting various diseases.

7   The fiber in green leaves help to clear your bowels. Having old, undigested food in your bowels is a major cause of ill health. When your colon is functioning properly, you have more energy!

Weight Loss

Your Natural Weight

Many people think they have to look like the slim ideals that exist in society and equate being thin with being happy. There are many tricks available to help us reach this so-called "ideal" weight including pills, powders, and different diets. However, these tricks exploit our desire to look "slim" without taking our energy, immune system, and happiness into account.

I want to replace the concept of "ideal" weight, which focuses on the external, with the concept of "natural" weight, which is achieved by changing your lifestyle and habits in such a way that you never again have to think about losing weight. When you have achieved your natural weight, you will

Green Smoothies Give You

BEAUTY

Clearer eyes
More radiant skin
Fresher breath
Stronger hair and nails
A flatter stomach and less cellulite
A positive glow

SPIRITUAL LIFE

Clearer, more positive thoughts
Stronger connection with your spirit
A gift to yourself and Mother Earth
Love for yourself
Feeling of calm and ease

WEIGHT

Improved digestion
Fewer cravings for unhealthy foods
Fiber to help the stomach stay healthy
Alkaline
Vital nutrients

LONGEVITY

Appearance and feeling of being ten years younger
Long-life and vitality
Healthy cells
A life filled with fun and laughterthis is essential for longevity
Nourishment for your whole being

be energetic, strong, powerful, as healthy as a horse, and happy. You will feel beautiful on the inside, and that shines through. Green smoothies can help you reach your natural weight and stay there. Green smoothies are satisfying; you won't have to go hungry, and you'll feel a sense of satisfaction that you might not have had before.

Happiness

Become happier!

The stomach and the intestines are directly linked to the brain and central nervous system. Therefore, they quickly react to what we do, eat, and feel. Some scientists call the stomach our second brain (read more about this in Michael Gershon's *The Second Brain*). About 95 percent of our "feel-good" hormone serotonin is activated by the stomach, and various gastrointestinal complaints are often related to stress. The green leaves that are the basis of green smoothies are rich in fiber. They also act as a sponge, by absorbing and removing undigested food and toxins that exist in our gut.

Sauerkraut juice is one of my favorite drinks and can be homemade (the recipe is on page 155) or purchased premade in the health food store. Sauerkraut contains plenty of the beneficial bacteria your stomach needs. To help the good bacteria in your stomach, you should drink sauerkraut juice or eat a tablespoon of sauerkraut or a fermented vegetable on a daily basis.

Sugar, flour, dairy, and animal products often make our bowels constipated and irritable, because they create a buildup of old, undigested food. The soluble fibers of the green smoothie help to clear the intestine. When you have a functioning gut, you become happier!

When we lose a few unwanted pounds, our bodies feel lighter. We automatically become happier, because we are evolving into the people we want to be. Green smoothies can help you get rid of cellulite, get a flatter stomach, stronger nails, and shinier hair. Your breath will become fresher and you will smell lovely. Because they help your skin to "tighten" and become smoother and more even, green smoothies can also make you look younger.

Introducing more pure food into your life can open up a doorway to your spiritual life. If you drink a green smoothie a day, you'll feel more in touch with yourself and may become more curious and open to discovering a new world within yourself. You will get to know yourself on a deeper level. You will no longer have to abuse food or try to push troublesome feelings aside with junk food and sugar. When you get in touch with yourself, you experience life with increased energy and pure joy.

Why a Miracle?

You might want to know what kind of miracle occurs whenever you start drinking green smoothies and juices. It's not a miracle that hits you like lightning, but a miracle that happens on the inside, quietly.

On wikipedia.com, a miracle is described as an "unexpected and sensational event, often regarded as a supernatural or divine intervention."

And that's exactly what it is. When you invite more green—living, nutritious food with the energy of light—into your life, a new energy is created, and you can feel and see things that you previously might not have felt or seen. Because we are usually so unaware of how vibrant life really is, this shift can seem supernatural.

I believe all human beings have their own divinity within themselves; however, not everyone can see their own divinity and live accordingly. One of the reasons we aren't in touch with our divinity is that many of us eat refined and processed products that divert energy from our consciousness and make us less capable of examining and discovering ourselves. The same applies to the stress of our daily schedule. Everything needs to be done quickly; we have to be the first, biggest, and the best, or we are nobody. Rather than looking at the beauty of the qualities that make us unique, we seek to be copies of one another. When we start looking at our own divinity with the help of raw food and green leaves, something awakens within us. We begin to look at ourselves as an entity in the universe and to take pride in the properties that make us unique. Imagine everyone as copies of each other. It's a pretty boring image, isn't it?

There is scientific research showing that every cell in our body has its own cosmos. When we sparkle with the joy of life and fill ourselves with the purest food, we let the cosmos flow through us, and small miracles begin to happen.

When we avoid stress-causing food such as caffeine, white sugar, and flour, a sense of calm starts to spread inside and out. That's when we discover that our actions contribute to the wellness of both the heart and the body. When we lose the pounds that we don't need, when the skin takes on a new luster, when the eyes begin to sparkle with the joy of life, when the whole body gets a positive glow—that's when our inner miracle manifests itself on the outside. By letting the miracle into your life, you will shine and bring inspiration to your fellow beings and encourage them to open up to miracles in their own lives. Let the miracle begin!

GREEN Smoothie Miracle

Raw Food and Green Smoothies

Green smoothies are raw foods. Raw foods are fruits, berries, root vegetables, vegetables, green leaves, nuts, seeds, dried fruit, cold-pressed oils, honey, seaweed, sprouts, some cereals, and superfoods that aren't cooked over 115 degrees. This means that all the nutrients, live enzymes, biophotons, and liquids in the food are preserved.

Minerals

Minerals are very important for the body to function at its optimum level. Minerals are natural elements that exist everywhere in nature and in the food we eat. Minerals help to build the skeleton. They are also a part of enzyme reactions, nerve signals, fluid regulations, and cell metabolism. Important minerals are: calcium and magnesium, which are both abundant in green leaves; sodium, which is found in celery; manganese, found in spinach; zinc and iron, found in parsley; potassium, which is in most vegetables; and selenium, found in the soil and in Brazil nuts.

Antioxidants

Antioxidants are substances or nutrients that prevent oxidation of our cells and act as the body's own internal anti-rust agent. Vitamins A, C, and E count as antioxidants.

The brighter the color of a vegetable or fruit, the more antioxidants it will contain. This also applies to something like green tea, which is loaded with antioxidants.

ORAC is a method of measuring the amount of antioxidants in food. A high ORAC value indicates a good source of antioxidants.

Phytochemicals give fruits, berries, and vegetables their color and are active in the immune system of plants. Different phytochemicals interact, and green smoothies contain a mixture of many different colors, making them full of antioxidants. The green in green leaves is chlorophyll that contains green vegetable dyes.

Phytochemicals protect the cells against free radicals. Free radicals are a by-product of metabolism and occur naturally in the body. However, if an imbalance occurs, there is a risk of excess free radicals circulating in our cells, and that's when we begin to age faster.

Live Enzymes

Live enzymes are small proteins that play a vital role in the digestive, metabolic, and immune systems. They help us remain strong and functional.

Live enzymes are found naturally in food; however, they are destroyed when heated. Therefore, cooked foods contain fewer vital enzymes. A lack of enzymes impairs digestion and the absorption of nutrients, can increase the amount of toxins in the body, and reduces protection against infections.

Because of its high content of enzymes and wealth of antioxidants, the raw food diet is commonly called the rejuvenation diet. When you eat raw, you feed your cells with the nutrients you need in order to live a long life. In an experiment performed on rats, those who were given a nutritious, low calorie diet lived longer than the rats that ate a "normal" diet. The conclusion was that humans could also live longer with this sort of diet. Instead of burdening our cells, this diet would strengthen them and help to create healthier and stronger new cells. If we fill our cells with live enzymes, we increase the potential of living a long and, hopefully, happy life. Where there is life, there are enzymes.

Biophotons are Lights

Biophotons are light energy that we can't always see but can subtly feel. In the 1920s, the Russian professor Alexander Gurwitsch noted that cells emit light and that this could affect cell division and the construction of living organisms. Gurwitsch also discovered the phenomenon of biophotons and described them as follows: "Biophotons are weak but coherent electromagnetic frequencies that are emitted by all living systems and that seem to be closely connected to the cell's physiological and biological functions as living things. All living creatures generate radiation. The body exudes biophotons, electromagnetic frequencies, heat, sound, and smell. The type of radiation directly depends on what condition the body is in . . . "

Biophotons (bio=life, photon=particle emitting light) can be made visible with the help of Kirlian photography. See pictures of Kirlian photography and read more about it in David Wolfe's book, *The Sunfood Diet Success System.*

Probiotics and Prebiotics—Vital life bacteria

Probiotics are lactic acid bacteria (beneficial bacteria) that are good for the intestinal flora and immune system. Probiotics have also proven to be good for different kinds of allergies. Beneficial bacteria live off the nutrients in the intestine, settling in the mucous membranes of the stomach and making it difficult for the harmful bacteria to access nutrients, or stick to the intestinal mucosa.

Probiotics are found in onions, garlic, cabbage, tomatoes, corn, and fermented foods like sauerkraut, kefir, yogurt, etc.

As all beneficial bacteria cannot reach the colon when they travel through the digestive system, we should consume probiotics daily in order to build and maintain a good balance in the intestinal tract.

Probiotics also help to produce vitamin K and the following B vitamins: B1, B2, B6, and B9 in the colon.

Prebiotics are oligosaccharide, a type of carbohydrate that the digestive system doesn't effectively break down, and which usually and ends up in the colon relatively unmetabolized. Prebiotics therefore contain a lot of healthy fiber and can be used as nourishment by beneficial bacteria. Probiotics can thrive in the gut if you add prebiotics to your diet. Prebiotics containing fructose-oligosaccharides, which are high in inulin, such as Yacon syrup, garlic, asparagus, and bananas, are particularly beneficial.

More About Raw Food

If you want to find out more about raw food, take a look at my book *Raw food—A Complete Guide for Every Meal of the Day.* Or, go online and watch videos about raw food on YouTube, or try to find out if there are other people in your town who like raw—anything that helps to get you started.

Victoria Boutenko—"The Green Smoothie Queen"

Victoria Boutenko has inspired thousands of people, including me. I call her "The Green Smoothie Queen." Victoria has written several books, including *Green for Life*, *Green Smoothie Revolution*, and *Raw family*.

Victoria and her family started eating raw food because of health issues and found that it helped them to overcome these issues. However, after about nine years of raw foods, Victoria and her family felt that something was wrong. Why were they so tired and unenergetic rather than happy and strong, like they were when they first started the diet? Victoria began researching the reasons for this disappointing turn of events, and she discovered that the DNA of human beings is 99.4 percent identical to that of chimps. She noticed how the chimpanzees ate large amounts of green leaves and started including these in her own diet. This led her to invent the green smoothie—a mixed drink that contains large amounts of greens and fruits in a form that allows the body to easily absorb all the healthy vitamins and minerals. After including green smoothies in their diet for a short while, Victoria and her family could feel their power and energy coming back.

Victoria also realized how few green leaves she and her family had eaten in the past, despite their raw food diet. Their raw diet had consisted primarily of nuts, seeds, and dried fruit. Victoria was so excited by what the green smoothies had done for her family, that she began to share her knowledge with others. People who tried the green smoothies lost weight, gained energy, and had fewer fast-food cravings. Today, Victoria travels the world and speaks of the vitality and joy that green smoothies bring.

"Green smoothies are the perfect start to the day."

Her amazing career at one of Manhattan's best PR agencies resulted in thirty extra pounds, bad skin, and bad moods. At that point, Filippa Svensson introduced raw food into her diet, which led her to the true meaning of life.

Eight years ago, I moved from Miami to New York to pursue a career in the Big Apple. After a week of interviews I was offered a job at one of Manhattan's top PR agencies. I was quickly thrown into a world where twelve-hour workdays with no lunch breaks and constant phone calls from customers were normal. I assumed this lifestyle was necessary in order to succeed. My unbalanced life started to reflect itself in my daily food intake, and I lived on sugar-free vanilla lattes, yogurt, ice cream, "healthy" whole grain chips with dip, chocolate covered raisins—anything that would give me quick energy and "help" me to cope with everyday stress. Three years later, I had gained thirty pounds, had skin breakouts, bad moods, and a constant lack of energy. I realized that I had become a different person. I didn't recognize myself. Americans have a very good saying that describes the situation I was in—"When you hit rock bottom, the only direction to go is up." At that moment, my life completely changed, and I realized that my health was more important than anything else, even my career. I visited a small local bookstore in Soho and bought a book about the basics of raw food, which I quickly read in one day. I never looked back. Since then, I have opened my own PR company, become a raw food blogger, and studied to become a holistic health coach at the Institute of Integrated Nutrition. Today, I realize that you can combine well-being and work and that you have to respect your body and its boundaries.

My raw food journey isn't just about food. It has opened my eyes to a whole new lifestyle that has made me find a clear direction in life and shown to me my true purpose. When I stopped pushing away my feelings of anxiety and discomfort, I suddenly discovered what I really felt, and I finally faced the unpleasant. These days, I follow my intuition when it comes to all choices, including breakfast, lunch, and dinner. My daily meals are based on love and respect for my body. My diet consists of 90 percent vegetables, fruits, nuts, and seeds, and 10 percent of "whatever I feel like at the moment." I think it's important to not focus too much on living 100 percent raw, and to allow yourself to listen to your inner signals and remain open

"My dream is for everyone to wake up and realize the importance of natural foods that the body recognizes."

Quick fact box:

Name: Filippa Svensson
Age: 29
Lives: New York
Family: Fiancée Stefan Salomonsson
Occupation: Runs the PR Agency LFB Media Group. Blogs for www.RawClarity.com and "Wellness" on Aftonbladet.se

to eating whatever you feel like in the moment. We are all different and we have to try different things—what works for me might not work for you, and vice versa. But one thing is clear: we all need green vegetables in our daily diet!

I want to know where my food comes from and what I am putting into my body—after all, this is what is going to build my new cells, and I always want to try to create a better, healthier Filippa. My dream is for everyone to wake up and realize the importance of natural food that the body recognizes. Natural food is easy to break down and contains lots of vitamins and minerals. According to Hippocrates's famous quote, "Let food be thy medicine, and medicine be thy food," food is a form of medicine. At every meal, we are faced with a choice; we can either build up the body or we can break it down.

Today I focus on living a balanced life where health is number one on my "to-do list." It requires constant planning and prioritization, but it's worth it! It took a while to adjust, but now it's a natural part of everyday life. I spend a lot of time on my body's internal well-being, which has given me external results, such as clear skin, shiny hair, stronger nails, reduced weight, and brighter eyes. In addition to this, I have stronger buds, my energy has increased, and I sleep better! I also make sure to exercise; preferably a nice jog along the Hudson River or a yoga class at Kundalini Yoga East in Union Square. Despite all the skepticism, it's actually fine to exercise on a raw diet. American raw food enthusiast Edwin Moses is a testament to this: he won Olympic gold in the 400-meter hurdles in 1976 and 1984. You go, Edwin!

Raw foodist and author Victoria Boutenko was my first inspiration. She gave me insight about the green smoothie and its benefits for the body. Victoria explained that green vegetables contain more valuable nutrients than any other food, and that the nutrients are stored in the cells of the plants. To release the nutrients, we must break down the cell walls, and the easiest way to do this is by mixing the green vegetables in a blender. This process helps your body absorb as much nutrition as possible.

My second role model, and the leader of the "green smoothie movement," is Kimberly Snyder. Nowadays, she is a health coach for Hollywood celebrities like Drew Barrymore and Hilary Duff, but prior to that, she was my yoga teacher at New York City Sports Club in the West Village. Her charisma and beautiful personality reflect her "Glowing Green Smoothie," a recipe that provides the body with lots of protein, fiber, vitamins, and minerals. It's a great energy-boosting drink, and Kimberly recommends you drink one every day.

I look at green smoothies and juices as natural vitamin boosters, which I really needed four years ago when I began my raw food journey. These days, my body needs at least one green smoothie a day. They reduce my cravings for "bad" food, especially sugar, because they provide the body with the nutrients it needs. Because of all the alkaline ingredients that go into a smoothie, such as spinach, banana, avocado, sprouts, and mango, green smoothies also help the body achieve the natural pH balance it's constantly striving to reach.

I always drink a green smoothie for breakfast, usually with some sort of natural fat, such as coconut oil, hemp seeds, flax seeds, pumpkin seeds, or avocado. I always include some sort of fruit, such as blueberries, raspberries, a banana, or a mango. I tend to feel a bit out of balance if I don't get my smoothie in the morning, just like coffee drinkers do when they don't get their daily dose of caffeine! Sometimes I have another smoothie in the afternoon, preferably "made with love" at one of my favorite places, One Lucky Duck or Organic Avenue. I usually stick to recipes that are based on 60:40, which means that 60 percent consists of organic fruit and 40 percent of organic green vegetables (also known as "greens"). The fruit flavor is dominant, and you can hardly taste the bitterness from the vegetables, but the bright green color is a sign that they're in the mixture. Most people love the drink once they get to taste the goodness and realize that it isn't dangerous. I've started to increase the proportion of green vegetables, as it makes my body feel good. I try to drink four to five cups a day.

Nowadays, I blog about the raw food lifestyle at RawClarity.com and on the wellness page at www.Aftonbladet.se. I'm grateful for all the knowledge I've gained in recent years, and I want to spread it through daily, inspirational in blog posts. I am also a holistic health coach. The word "holistic" refers to wholeness, and that's exactly how I look at health and the body. We must make ourselves "whole" again. I teach my clients how to see that everything is connected and help them to put the puzzle pieces of their lives back together, including their relationship to food.

A part of my heart still burns for PR, but today, I choose my clients, pace, and working hours. This has given me a healthier, more peaceful, and happier life. For me, it's about taking control of the parts of life that you can control and letting go of the parts that you cannot.

My favorite recipe:

"Mix together 2 handfuls of organic spinach, 1 organic banana, and 2 cups of water or natural coconut water."

My top advice on how to try green smoothies:

"For beginners, it may be easier to drink green smoothies with more fruit, so that sweet taste dominates. Combine banana, mango, and pineapple, or add a little honey, stevia, or agave."

Why I drink green smoothies:

"Because of the natural vitamin high, the positive impact on the balance of the body, and the reduced sugar cravings."

Funniest comment someone made when telling them about green smoothies:

"A friend asked if I ever occasionally get the urge to pick the leaves off the trees so that I can add them to the green smoothies. I love nature, but I prefer to buy my vegetables at the store or in the local market."

I drink my smoothies:

"For breakfast in the morning and as an afternoon snack."

Why, What, How, When, Where Green Smoothies?

Why Drink Green Smoothies?

- Green smoothies give your digestive system a break from ordinary food, which leads to increased energy.
- You automatically and significantly reduce your oil and salt intake.
- When you drink two to three cups (500–750 ml) of green smoothies daily, you get enough greens to nourish your body, and all of the beneficial nutrients are well absorbed.
- The chlorophyll boosts you and your cells you shine more.
- It's an investment in your health.
- You might lose some unnecessary extra pounds and reach your natural weight.
- Your eyes begin to sparkle.
- You oxygenate the body and provide it with calcium, chlorophyll, liquid, and vitality through biophotons and live enzymes.

What is a Green Smoothie?

- A nutritious drink that's composed of green leaves, fruit, and water. The proportions of the drink are optimal for humans, as 60 percent of the drink consists of organic, ripe fruit and 40 percent of green leaves.
- A drink "invented" by Victoria Boutenko.
- Similar to what the chimpanzees eat and "thrive on."

How to make a Green Smoothie?

What you need:

- Green leaves, fruit, water.
- A cutting board and a knife.
- A colander or a salad spinner for rinsing your green leaves.
- A glass, bottle, or thermos, if you want your smoothie to go.
- A blender. There are many different kinds of blenders, and they range widely in price and strength. Once you get started with your smoothies, it's worth investing in a blender that's a little more expensive. It will be quicker and stronger, and it will allow you to crush frozen fruit and berries, which are included in the delicious green ice cream smoothies.

When to Have Green Smoothies?

- Breakfast—for the best start to your day. If you travel to work by car, bus, or subway, it's easy to bring your smoothie with you.
- Snack—instead of a coffee, refuel with the real and easy energy of a smoothie.
- Lunch—a quick lunch that's easy to carry.
- Before and after exercise—the perfect workout meal. Feel free to boost your smoothie with rice or hemp protein powder after a workout.
- Dinner—feels good for the body and enables it to rest overnight. The smoothie doesn't burden the system as much as a "regular" dinner, so it's fine to drink it a little later at night. If you work nights, it's the perfect way for the body to get digestible nutrients and food that passes through the body quickly.

It's not about replacing all your meals with a green smoothie. A friend of mine started to replace her morning sandwich with a smoothie. The rest of the day she ate as she normally would. If you eat five meals a day, this means it's a 25 percent improvement in your overall diet. If you want to undergo a cleanse, you can replace all your meals with a green smoothie. Learn more about detox on page 55.

Where to Have a Green Smoothie?

- A green soup is the perfect appetizer or a light dinner.
- At a picnic.
- With friends.
- While you're waiting for the subway.
- You can drink a smoothie at anywhere and at any time!

Green Smoothies All Year 'Round!

Yes, you can drink green smoothies all year round; you just have to adjust the fruit and veggies you use according to the season. When you vary green leaves, fruits, and berries according to the season, the flavors are tastier and more intense and the nutrient content will be higher.

The Importance of Variation

Green leaves contain tiny amounts of alkaloids, a group of organic chemical compounds that are primarily found in seed plants. It's the plant's protection against being eaten. Alkaloids are fat-soluble and are easily absorbed by the body through the mucous membranes and the skin. In small doses, they have strong positive effects on the human body, as they strengthen the immune system and make the body more alkaline.

It's not good to ingest too much alkaloid. Therefore, it's important to vary the green leaves. This usually happens naturally, as the supply of green leaves varies according to the season.

Spring

Wild green leaves begin to sprout: spruce shoots, birch leaves, purslane, stinging nettles, etc. Varieties of lettuce grown in greenhouses are available for purchase.

Summer

Wild green leaves are growing in nature. Lettuces grown in the open land are available in stores. Black currant and raspberry leaves are growing in the garden.

Pick and freeze seasonal berries.

Fall

Harvest time! There are still a lot of wild leaves available in the fall, and the farmer's market usually has a wide selection of swiss chard as well as different varieties of kale and zucchini.

Winter

Kale, cabbage, and frozen green leaves.
You may need a heavier smoothie with more fat and/or warming spices, tea, or miso base.
Fresh spices are available all year round and are a delicious addition to greens.
Green alfalfa sprouts turn into chlorophyll and are a good source of nutrition in winter.

Where to Buy

From the wild—it's free, organic, and locally produced!
Farmers' market—you'll be able to buy your green leaves directly from the grower.
Organic shop—the best option if you have to buy green leaves from a store.

Various Leaves

1. Green smoothies are best when made from wild leaves and edible flowers that you pick yourself. Examples of these can be found in the table on page 34.
2. A produce salad that you pick from the garden.
3. Organic lettuce grown in pots that you buy from the organic store.
4. Organic salads.
5. Organic salad bags.
6. Frozen organic leaves.

Why Organic?

1. Organic farming protects our water.
2. The balance of nature is not affected in an unnatural way.
3. The earth gets the chance to remineralize itself and rest between harvests. Our earth needs to recover, just like you and me. You can't run a marathon every day.
4. The farmers who grow the primary products are healthy and don't have to work with pesticides.

If you choose organic, you're not just doing a good deed for your fellow human beings and our earth, you are also getting the best and most nutritious produce available.

Good to Know!

It's the roots that provide the leaf with nutrients from the soil. The moment the leaf is picked and the connection with the root is broken, the nutritional value of the leaf begins to deteriorate.

"I was basically addicted to freshly squeezed juice when I was living in Los Angeles."

GREEN Smoothie

"The body longs for chlorophyll"

Andreas Wilson is an actor who alternates between a theatrical career and standing behind a counter and squeezing juice at his own juice bar, Juiceverket.

I tried my first green smoothie in Los Angeles, where there were juice bars on every corner. I mainly hung out at the Beverly Hills Juice Bar, and I basically became addicted to freshly-squeezed juice while I was living there.

After living in California, I decided to set up my own non-alcoholic cocktail bar in my hometown of Stockholm. I met some friends who shared my vision; we decided to go for it and opened the juice bar Juiceverket.

One bar evolved into two. Sure, it can be tough at times to combine acting with squeezing juice, but I don't have to record or participate in theater performances everyday. Sometimes I have a lot of things to think about, and that's when I have to bite the bullet and work efficiently. For me, it's both stimulating and beneficial to work on different things.

Acting is such a competitive and uncertain profession, so the two jobs complement each other. My dream is to keep things the way they are now, and I hope I don't ever have to choose between the juice bar and the theater.

Quick fact box:

Name: Andreas Wilson
Age: 31
Lives: Stockholm, Södermalm
Family: Married
Occupation: Actor and Juice Maker
Working on: Constantly starring in various movies and theatrical productions. Will continue to develop Juiceverket and www.juiceverket.se.

My interest in food and drink stems from a curiosity about how the things I put into my body affect me. In addition, exercise is a big part of my life, and for the most part, I live a life that has a positive effect on my health. However, I wouldn't call myself a health freak.

As an actor, it's important to stay in shape in order to be strong enough to deal with the fast pace and to feel good. When you live an intense life and work with different projects under a deadline, it's also important to get as much nutrition as possible. And green drinks are one of the best ways I know. That's when it's good to have your own juice bar.

There's something delightful about green drinks. It's like the body craves chlorophyll. For us at Juiceverket, it's always important that our drinks taste good. The fact that they are healthy is a side benefit. I think one is more likely to continue to drink green if it tastes good. At the moment, I'm very fond of peas and spinach.

My favorite recipe:
"Coralldo Pick-Me-Up: celery, spinach, lemon with zest, apple, beetroot, broccoli, and one teaspoon of Pukka Vitalise, a lyophilized powder made from brussels sprouts."

Why I drink green smoothies:
"Because they provide tremendous amounts of energy and nutrients in a simple and tasty way."

I drink my smoothies:
"Whenever I feel like it, which is one of the advantages of having your own juice bar."

CREATE YOUR OWN GREEN SMOOTHIE FAVORITES

GREENS	SWEET FRUIT	SOUR FRUIT	SWEETE-NERS	SUPER-FOODS	CREAMY TEXTURE	LIQUID BASE
Wild green leaves: e.g., stinging nettles, purslane, miners lettuce.	Pear	Lime	Stevia	Green powders	Soaked dried fruits	Tulsi tea
Kale	Apple	Lemon	Dates	Spirulina	Banana	Chaga tea
Spinach	Mango	Grape	Soaked dried fruit (e.g., figs, apricots)	Nettle powder	Avocado	Green tea
Arugula	Banana	Pome-granate	Banana	Hemp protein powder	Ripe pear	Yerba mate
Watercress	Pine-apple	Orange	Lucuma	Camu camu	Mango	Apple juice
Lettuce	Melon		Honey	Sunwarrior protein powder	Apricot	Orange juice
Celery	Papaya		Mesquite	Raw cacao	Soaked chia seeds	Coconut water
Broccoli	Peaches			Maca powder	Soaked flax seeds	
Cucumber				Baoba		
Zucchini				Açaí		
Bok choy				Fresh or frozen berries		
Carrot & beetroot tops						
Chard						
Spinach						
Fresh herbs (e.g., dill, basil, cilantro, parsley)						
Sprouts						
Wild edible flowers						

Green leaves: Preferably choose wild leaves that you can pick yourself. Choose green leaves and edible wild flowers according to season.

Fruits: Can be categorized as sweet or sour. To avoid the wrong dietary combinations, don't mix sweet and sour fruits.

Berries: Are neutral and can be used in various combinations.

Sweeteners: The fruit itself is sweet, which means there's usually no need to add sweetners. However, if you would like to add extra sweetener, follow the suggestions in the sweeteners column.

Superfoods: You can experiment with these to boost the green smoothies and to find more variations that you like.

Creamy texture: We are all different and we like our green smoothies to have various consistencies. If you want to make your smoohies creamier, you can try adding the ingredients in this column.

Liquid base: Water is usually used as the liquid base, but the items in this column can add more power to the smoothie and give it a more distinctive taste.

Three Ways to Eat More Greens—Salad, Smoothie, and Juice

There are three ways to eat more greens. Try them all to determine what works for you.

Salad

How delightful, a large, fresh, green salad, with a creamy salad dressing! It's one of my favorite meals, and I prefer it with lots of parsley as a base. Gabriel Cousens, one of the first and foremost proponents of raw food, thinks we should eat green salads to activate our masticatory function, and that in chewing, we are "unfolding the hidden message in the food." Chewing each bit slowly, deliberately, and for a long time makes us experience the food with all our senses. A salad is often very pretty and inviting. When we eat a salad, it's essential that we spend time with the food, that we chew and enjoy, in order to facilitate digestion and give our bodies the opportunity to absorb the nutrition.

Smoothie

In order to assimilate most of the nutrients in food, we need to chew thoroughly, and sometimes we may not have the time. In these situations, green smoothies offer an ideal way of ingesting the green leaves. Digestion begins in your mouth, actually a bit before that—as soon as we start thinking of the food we are about to eat, the enzymes that break down the food are produced.

When you drink a green smoothie, the blender helps the chewing process, and the body isn't required to convert the food into nutrition.

The advantage of green smoothies is that you can consume larger quantities of green leaves and thereby increase the intake of nutrients.

Juice

In green juices, all fibers have been removed, which makes them very cleansing. It's said that juices put the least amount of strain on the body and therefore help the body heal. Because green juices contain very little fruit—at most, the equivalent of an apple—they also cleanse the intestines and allow us to "reset" our cells, preventing sugar cravings or the "composting effect," which some research shows is caused by sugar. The composting effect causes the body and its cells to age more quickly than they should. When you drink green juices, there is no need to chew, all you have to do is drink. Often, you will experience an instantaneous energy boost, as the juice reaches the cells directly. It's like taking a shortcut past the digestive system. Use a juice extractor when you make your green juices. Learn more about how to make green juices on page 24.

Digestion

Our digestive system uses about 70 percent of our total energy, and by drinking smoothies and juices, we facilitate digestion. Given the stress that exists today, a lot of our energy is used to "escape" or save ourselves from that stress. This means that we have less energy left to digest food. We may not be able to assimilate the nutrients in all the great foods we eat. By blending a smoothie or a juice, we help the digestive system assimilate important nutrients the body needs.

FIVE REASONS TO LOVE GREEN SMOOTHIES

1. Quick to make.
2. Will make you shine.
3. Convenient to carry.
4. Super nutritious.
5. Keep you slim and full of energy.

Food Nourishment Combinations/Acid-Base Balance

The Perfect Food Combination

One way to good health is to combine various ingredients correctly, since they vary in how long they take to digest. We are all sensitive in different ways, and it's important to find the combinations that give each of us energy and strength.

Green leaves are *not* a vegetable. They cannot be compared to vegetables such as cabbage, broccoli, and carrots, which all contain a lot of fiber and a type of starch. Because green foods don't contain starch, you can combine them with all kinds of nutrients. This means that practically every green smoothie has an ideal composition that will promote your health in the best possible way. However, to facilitate further digestion and absorption of nutrients, a smoothie should really contain as few ingredients as possible. Drink the smoothie by itself, and wait for thirty minutes before eating anything else.

Drinking your green smoothie is more important than *how* you make it.

Acid-Base Balance

Green leaves are basic. You can tell if a food is basic by how many minerals it contains. It's the balance between the acid-forming minerals—chlorine, sulfur, and phosphorus—and the base-forming minerals—potassium, calcium, magnesium, and sodium—that determines whether a food is acid- or base-forming. Choosing your diet according to these minerals is also known as the alkaline diet. The acidity in our bodies is measured by the so-called pH value. Our blood is perfectly balanced at a pH value of 7.365, and the body is constantly working to keep itself at this level. When our blood is acidic, we experience inflammation, swelling, and fatigue.

Pain in the joints, sugar cravings, acne, bad breath, and headaches can be a sign that your blood pH level is too acidic. You can measure the pH value of your urine and saliva at home using litmus paper, which may be purchased at your health food store. Do a test every morning for a week, and you'll get a good idea of your pH balance. When your diet becomes less acidic, your pH balance becomes more basic. When your pH balance becomes more basic, your cravings for sweets, junk food, caffeine, and alcohol fade. It's a simple way to invest in your health.

Chlorophyll is what gives the green leaf its color, and the richer the leaves are in chlorophyll, the more base-forming power they have. When we help the body to become more basic, the body cleansing organs don't have to work as hard. It is even said that the more basic you are, the less risk you have of suffering from various diseases and other difficulties such as hay fever and eczema. The easiest way to eat more alkaline is to eat more leafy greens, green smoothies, salads, or green juices.

It's not only food that can affect your pH value; thoughts, stress levels, your breathing, and your outlook on life are also relevant factors. By thinking more positively and feeling more love and compassion, you can make yourself more basic.

What do our cells need to thrive?

When we get hungry, we often just focus on filling our stomachs with food. We forget to think about what our bodies really need. For the cells to function optimally, it's our job to help them in the process of producing new cells or repairing old ones. When we feed our cells quantities of food and don't pay attention to the quality, the cells continue to cry for nutrition. In other words, our cells are still starving, even though the stomach is full. That's why it's important to start thinking of the quality of the food we eat.

Our trillions of cells continuously work to absorb nutrients and to repair and renew themselves. Undigested or partially digested food may increase the normal level of waste in the body. That is, waste products such as chemicals from food, water, the environment, and medications, increase. The waste is collected throughout the body in organs, tissues, cells, and the space between the cells. When the body is in balance, the waste is minimized, and eventually the lymph removes it.

Fatigue is often a sign of high toxicity in the body and can become a vicious cycle—fatigue releases toxins, which perpetuate fatigue. Stress and tension also release toxins in the body. A surplus of toxicity may arise in our cleansing organs and the tissue space between the cells. This excess affects our health, our energy levels, and our figure. That's when a thorough cleansing of the body at a cellular level is needed to help improve system performance. At this stage, a detox is needed. Read more about detox on page 55.

Lymph is the fluid that surrounds the body's cells and constitutes the cells "inner environment." We wouldn't survive very long in a heavily polluted environment if it wasn't for lymph.

The lymphatic system is also called the body's "garbage collector," which is easy to understand since the lymphatic system cleanses the body. But that's just one aspect of it. The lymphatic system serves many other functions, including acting as a protective guard against infections and diseases.

Unlike the blood, which is regulated by the heart, the lymph has no central pump. In order for the lymph to function optimally, muscle contraction (which occurs during exercise) and deep breathing must also take place.

In order for the cells to get nourishment and for the tissue to stay healthy, smooth, and firm, the exchange of nutrients and waste must happen uninterrupted and unhindered.

When the flow of the lymph is jammed, excess fluid piles up in the tissue. In areas where the circulation is poor, the liquid usually ends up in the hips and thighs, which results in cellulite. Poor lymphatic circulation also results in fatigue and inertia; this makes the human susceptible to disease and cell destruction which may lead to premature aging. We should invest heavily in effective lymphatic function, not just to avoid cellulite but to protect our health in general.

This is why it's so important to eat food that's clean and toxin free and to exercise, so that the lymph can do its job efficiently and allow us to shine.

Breathing

Oxygen is our cells' primary need. The more oxygenated our cells, the less our risk of imbalance and disease. We oxygenate our cells by breathing. It's also by breathing that we help the body eliminate waste products and toxins. We take about 25,000 breaths a day, and breathing is an automatic process that follows our thoughts, feelings, and physical body. As we become more aware of our breathing and how it affects our lives, we can practice awareness of our breath. We strive for calm, harmonious, and deep breathing. When we breathe deeply, the diaphragm gets a workout, which directly impacts the lymphatic system and helps the body get rid of old waste.

A Simple Exercise for Deep Breathing: Exhale thoroughly and empty the lungs of oxygen. Inhale through the nose for four counts, hold your breath for twelve counts, and then exhale through the nose for eight counts. Repeat ten times. Remember, your stomach should inflate as you inhale and deflate as you exhale.

Water

We need a good fluid balance in order to feel healthy. Drinking one fluid ounce per two pounds of body weight a day is recommended. Water is a key component of our body and is needed for the body to function correctly. Water is necessary for the transfer of nutrients and oxygen to the cells, regulation of body temperature, blood transportation, and for a healthy pH value. Water helps us stay concentrated and gives us stamina. It is also integral to the body's natural purification system. Around 70 percent of our body consists of water, and if we're below that number, that means we're dehydrated. If we're dehydrated, symptoms such as headaches, sore joints, constipation, and fatigue may occur. The water we drink must be of high quality. Spring water is the optimal drink. You can improve tap water by filtering it through a pitcher or by fitting a special filter to the kitchen faucet. However, when you filter water, some vital minerals get lost; so, don't forget to add mineral drops and a little bit of salt to recrystallize the water.

> ## TIP
>
> To clear out and make your body more alkaline, start every morning with one and a half to two glasses (300-500 ml) of water with lemon.

Food

When the cells are provided with enough oxygen and water, we can add nutrients in the form of food. For best quality, choose organic, unrefined foods that are as natural as possible—it will make your cells cheer. In order for the body to clean itself, we need to eat foods that are rich in fiber. Green leaves are rich in fiber. Fiber functions like a kind of magnet in the body by attracting toxins and undigested food in the intestine. Without fiber, the toxins would remain in the body. We ingest toxins from different sources, including the environment in which we live, heavy metals, pesticides from the foods we eat, undigested food, and debris from the rebirth of cells. We can help the body by consuming a high fiber diet.

Ingredients

Açaí	—a small, dark purple berry with a flavor that suggests a mixture of chocolate and blueberry. It is one of the berries with the highest ORAC value (a method of measuring the amount of antioxidants found in various foods). It's the perfect thing to eat if you're coming down with a cold. It's also perfect for enhancing green smoothies.
Arugula	—has a unique, spicy taste and is rich in vitamins A and C, iron, and calcium.
Basil	—traditionally used for problems with the heart, breathing, joints, eyes, and skin. Basil can also support the immune system and help fight everyday stress.
Bok Choy	—is incredibly rich in nutrients and has crisp, light green stems and green leaves similar to spinach. Widely used in Asian cooking.
Camu Camu	—a small, red berry with the nickname "nature's vitamin pill." It contains more vitamin C than any other food, as well as loads of antioxidants, vitamins, and minerals. It's good for your heart, brain, eyes, liver, and skin, and it's also a real boost for the immune system.
Celery	—contains naturally bitter substances that stimulate the digestion. It's rich in potassium, calcium, and magnesium. These three minerals can help lower blood pressure as well as make the body more alkaline.
Chaga tea	—a medicinal mushroom that grows mainly on birches and is full of antioxidants! It has one of the highest ORAC values among foods. (a method of measuring the amount of antioxidants found in various foods). It's also said to strengthen the body, fight stress and fatigue, and improve metabolism and mental capacity. Chaga is available in powder form or in portions used for brewing tea. You can add the powder right into your smoothie or make tea and use that as a base for your green smoothie.

Chia	—a little seed that consists of 20 percent omega-3 fatty acids, a higher percentage than both salmon and flax seed. This makes the chia seed the best omega-3 source available. In addition, it contains more calcium than milk and 30 percent more antioxidants than blueberries. It's often eaten soaked, as it turns into a jelly.
Chlorella	—an alga that's extremely detoxifying, as it binds and clears out heavy metals and other harmful substances from the body. It also helps friendly bacteria like lactobacillus multiply quickly, which is very good for digestion. You can eat chlorella in tablet or powder form.
Cilantro	—cleanses the body of mercury, aluminum, and lead.
Citrus fruits	—contain high levels of vitamin C. Lemons are diuretic and help to create a basic environment in the body. Besides containing large amounts of vitamin C, oranges also contain a lot of potassium and calcium.
Cacao	—the cacao bean is called the "food of the Gods" and is one of the richest in antioxidants. It contains the amino acid tryptophan, which affects serotonin levels in the body and makes us feel happy and in love!
Cucumber	—consists of 96 percent water and provides excellent hydration to our cells. Also contains dietary fiber and vitamin C.
Dried fruit	—figs, apricots, raisins, etc. Soak for 2–4 hours before you use them to add a creaminess and sweetness to smoothies. Dates with seeds are fresh and don't need to be soaked.
Flax	—a seed that's rich in omega 3 and 6. When it comes in contact with water it turns into a jelly, which contains a great deal of fiber. It's therefore good to eat flax seeds if you're constipated.
Ginger	—a rhizome with an aromatic and spicy flavor. It has been used in India and China for thousands of years to treat stomach problems, fevers and infections and to promote vitality and long life. Ginger can also be used for motion sickness or a cold, as it relieves nasal congestion and opens up the sinuses. Ginger also heats you up from the inside.

Green powder	—there are many different kinds of green powder including spirulina, chlorella, nettles, wheat grass, and barley grass powder. You can add these to your smoothie or just dissolve the powder into a glass of water and drink. They're a good addition in the winter, when it can be hard to get hold of fresh green leaves.
Green tea	—has a high content of antioxidants and protects against several diseases. It also increases the metabolism and is said to promote weight loss.
Hemp protein powder	—is one of the best plant-based protein sources. It contains all the essential amino acids as well as the important fatty acids omega 3, 6, and 9, which are great for luster of the skin, hair and eyes. It's an excellent addition for anyone who exercises a lot.
Lúcuma	—has a sweet caramel taste that is somewhat reminiscent of maple syrup. It's therefore a very good sweetener. Unlike other sweeteners, lúcuma has a low sugar content.
Maca	—a root from Peru, which is used to increase stamina and improve our performance, among other things. It's also said to have a positive effect on sexual desire and is therefore known as "The Peruvian Viagra."
Mesquite	—a pod that's very nutritious. It has a sweet taste but doesn't make the blood sugar unstable. It has a low glycemic index, which means it takes longer for the body to break down than sugar. Works well as a sweetener.
Miner's lettuce	—a green leaf with a crunchy, mild taste. Packed with vitamins A and C and iron.
Nettle	—a very nutritious herb that's good for the stomach, intestinal problems, throat complaints, urinary tract disorders, and rheumatic problems.
Nettle powder	—a very nutritious powder that's good for stomach and intestinal problems, throat complaints, urinary tract disorders, and rheumatic problems.
Parsley	—great for urinary tract infections and the stimulation of milk production in nursing women. Rich in vitamin C, iron, and minerals. It's also a good breath freshener.

Purslane	—a green leaf with a slightly sour and salty taste. It's an excellent source of vitamin A, which is essential for good vision and very good for the skin.
Spinach	—a super-food that's high in antioxidants, vitamins A, C, K, and B9, and folic acid. It's good for the immune system and hypertension, and it's also said to increase stamina.
Spirulina	—a blue-green alga called "the miracle alga." It consists of 60–70 percent protein and contains lots of vitamins, minerals, and chlorophyll. It's said to be immune system-enhancing, antiviral, and a protectant against cancer.
Sprouts	—contains all substances it needs during the first week of its life. The nutrients are therefore unusually absolute and concentrated compared to those of other vegetables.
Stevia	—a shrub. The leaves are pulverized and used as a sweetener. It doesn't contain any calories, has a zero GI, and does not affect the blood sugar. Nutritionally, it's rich in essential oils, vitamins, enzymes, and minerals. In addition, it is said to kill bacteria that cause tooth decay.
Sunwarrior protein powder	—a vegan protein powder derived from sprouted brown rice. It has a protein content of 85 percent and contains all the essential amino acids. The powder also helps the body absorb vitamins and minerals more efficiently.
Tulsi tea	—one of the main herbs in Ayurvedic medicine, it has been used for its health benefits for thousands of years. Among other things, it is used to prevent stress and boost the immune system. It's also classified as an adaptogen. Adaptogens increase the body's ability to adapt to what you need; If you need to become calmer, it can help you to relax; if you need to become livelier, it can give you more energy.

Yerba mate —South America's answer to coffee. Because of its caffeine content, it provides the same stimulating effect as coffee, but its chemical composition is said to remove some of the negative effects of caffeine. This means that many don't experience the nervousness and anxiety that they may experience after drinking coffee. The stomach is not affected in the same way, either. Yerba mate is said to stimulate digestion and the production of bile, increase fat metabolism, raise the body temperature, and boost energy levels when mental and physical fatigue occur.

"It feels like I drank my first green smoothie with gruel."

"I am a smoothie freak"

For yoga devotee Malin Berghagen, yoga and green smoothies are the parts of life that strengthen and bring energy, awareness, and peace.

Health has always been my trademark. As a child, I was called the little witch, because of the various herbal concoctions I made whenever someone was ill. As a twelve-year-old, I started visiting health clinics, and nowadays, I still work at a health clinic called Masegården a couple of times a year. Taking care of my shrine comes naturally to me; it's my body that I live in. But it hasn't always been like that. Modern times demand that we look and act in a certain way, especially for us women. That's why I travel to different places in Sweden to give lectures and courses to help others take the same actions as I do and start living a healthier life. I have the courage to stay strong, as a woman, a mother, and a human being.

Having two famous parents, I was born into the world of artists. I was in a photo shoot when I was only six hours old. I worked as a model early on, and in my teens, I visited both Paris and Tokyo. I subsequently chose to work in the magical world of theater, which wasn't much of a surprise to me. It was very relaxing. Well, that might be a bit of a lie, as being on stage

---

Quick fact box:

Name: Malin Berghagen

Age: 46

Lives: Stockholm

Family: My children Christopher, Love, Linn, and Isak, fiancée Martin, and my dog Bodhi.

Occupation: Yoga teacher, lecturer, motivator, and writer. Blogs for Kings and Angels, www.kingsandangels.se, and is a co-owner of Mamita Sthlm, www.mamitasthlm.se.

Working on: Several yoga trips with Springtime, www.springtime.se, courses at Masesgården, www.masesgarden.se, Sweden's only traditional health clinic, and writing a personal book on yoga.

can be far from relaxing, but it's a pretty cool experience once you have the courage to face your nerves. To be afraid, but to stubbornly overcome that feeling, can be incredibly powerful. I also love to challenge and be challenged by my colleagues, and I love what we create together. This experience helped me to earn a theater award. To me, theater isn't just about acting; it's really about meetings with my colleagues, the audience, and myself. During my teens, I started practicing yoga regularly, but in my late teens I took a break from it. Twenty years later, I was given a yoga class as a gift from a friend and met my yoga teacher, Maria Boox. I realized how much I had missed yoga, and it reconquered my heart.

My yoga teacher, Maria Boox, is my greatest inspiration; another, in fact, is Erica's husband, Sam. He always gives me good yoga vibes. He doesn't know it, but he really does. After hanging out with Erica and Sam for a day, I want to do yoga even more.

Yoga has provided me with tools that have helped me in life and given me courage to explore all that I am. The respect I have for my body has been strengthened, and today, I like myself on the inside as well. Yoga has also helped take my acting to another level. It helps me stay focused and dare to be in silence. It allows me to be consciously present. Yoga helps me stay present in life in general. It keeps my body healthy, flexible, and strong, and I have learned to not take anyone or anything for granted.

Practicing regularly is something that comes naturally to me, but I never spend two hours in a row on my mat. Instead, I practice for shorter periods throughout the day.

To me, green smoothies are also a part of life, and it feels like I was drinking my first green smoothie with gruel. I'm a smoothie freak, and I could live entirely off such drinks.

I consume at least one green smoothie a day. They're a great way to start the morning or end the night, especially if I'm peckish for something.

I have a lot of favorites, but I especially like a green smoothie Erica told me about, which contains celery, cucumber, and green apple. It's really a great start to the morning!

Many people have asked me why I do so many different things. I never really understood that question, because the things I do are just parts of who I am. I always try to work with what lies closest to me, because this is where my knowledge lies and what interests me. Actor and director Figge Norling once called me an artist of life, and I very much like that statement. Yes, I am an artist of life, I want to create my own life and grasp the possibilities that are there. To break free and dare to be innovative, yet stay within the areas that interest me, is extremely stimulating. Currently, I am combining yoga trips around Sweden and the world with writing a personal book about yoga.

My favorite recipe:

"Green leaves, avocado, banana, coconut water, and lots of blueberries."

My best advice on how to get started with green smoothies:

"Just do it! Add cold apples and lemons to your fruit extractor. Add a bit of ginger. Yummy! Tip: vary with celery, cucumber, parsley, and cold orange juice."

Why I drink my green smoothies:

"Because they're delicious and healthy."

The funniest comment someone made about my green smoothies:

"My son Isak: 'No mom, I don't want to eat flowers!! '"

I drink my smoothies:

"Usually for breakfast or as a snack."

Green Smoothie Cleanse/Detox

If you are looking to undergo a detox, green smoothies are the perfect diet. Choose any number of days, but if consuming a liquid-only diet is something you've never experienced before, start with one to three days. This ensures that the cleansing doesn't happen too quickly and allows you to avoid nausea, headaches, and fatigue. You may experience less-than-pleasant symptoms on your cleanse if you are a habitual coffee drinker or eat white sugar or other simple carbs regularly.

Benefits of a green leaf detox:

- You don't have to experience hunger.
- You get to chew.
- The fiber in green leaves promotes good bowel movements and the stomach will behave.
- Smoothies with fruit satisfy sugar cravings.
- Avocado adds substance and creaminess to the drink.

Things to remember:

1. Prepare the body by cutting down on caffeine, animal products, and simple carbs for a few days to a week before you start the detox in order to reduce the physical symptoms.
2. Stay in the same mind frame when you finish the cleanse by gradually eating the types of food you were eating before the detox. Introduce one food at a time and see how it makes your body feel. Food you were eating before might not taste good anymore or may even make your body feel uncomfortable.
3. If you wish to clear the bowels you can use enemas or visit a colon-cleansing specialist.
4. Smoother skin, brighter eyes, increased energy, alertness, weight loss, and a happy gut are just a few of the benefits of the treatment.

My One-Week Green Smoothie Cleanse

One day I was browsing on YouTube, trying to find stories about how green smoothies have helped people. I was so inspired by all the stories, I decided to try a green drink detox for a week. Here is my diary from that week.

Day One

I stocked up on lots of wonderful ingredients such as arugula, spinach, lettuce, fruits, and berries. In order to succeed with a purification week, I realized I needed to have a fridge filled with delicious ingredients to make the purification simple and straightforward. I also bought some tetra pak sauerkraut juice, in case I didn't have the time to make my own smoothie. It's always good to have a backup of bottled green juices or green powder.

After my morning yoga, I was a little extra-hungry for breakfast, so I had a fruit porridge made of celery stalks and apple.

I had already used the sauerkraut juice and tetra pak vegetable soup. I was sitting in front of the computer and lost track of time, then rushed to pick up my daughter, Saga, from her grandmother's house and drive her to swimming class.

That afternoon, after standing ouside for two hours, I needed something to warm me up. When I got home, I made carob tea, and to satisfy my sweet cravings, I added some chia seeds, which are incredibly nutritious. They also help to keep the intestines in good shape, which is very important during a cleanse.

When it was time to cook my green dinner of the day, I got excellent help from my four-year-old daughter. I felt that my blood sugar was low and couldn't wait too long to eat, but Saga made dinner on her own, under my supervision. This is going well, I thought. Just then, Saga accidentally knocked over the 1.5 quarts of green smoothie, and it was all over the kitchen. I almost started to cry. I sat down for a few minutes and breathed. I took out the dish cloth, paper, and a good mood. That evening, I was a little hungry and already missed chewing on something. But my stomach felt fine and I felt energetic. I also went to the toilet a few times extra during the day, which strikes me as a good sign.

Exercise: Yoga 90 minutes

6:00 AM ⅕ cup wheat grass juice (read more about wheat grass on page 157)
8:30 AM 2 scoops of Sunwarrior protein powder
9:45 AM Fruit porridge
1:00 PM One tetra pak (3 cups) of vegetable soup
3:30 PM 2 cups of sauerkraut juice
5:00 PM 1 tablespoon chia seeds soaked in carob tea plus 1 tablespoon honey
7:30 PM 2.5 cups green smoothie

Day Two

The day began at four o'clock in the morning. I had to buy some groceries for the raw food course I'd be teaching the next day. I had a wheat grass shot early in the morning and brought along a cup of tulsi tea that warmed me after shopping for luscious fruits and vegetables. I had the same morning porridge as the day before, and it turned out to be an excellent breakfast for a four-year-old girl, too. I had breakfast at a "normal" time of the day, but since I had already been awake for quite a few hours, I was soon hungry again. It can be a bit tricky to be strict during a detox, especially when you have children who may not really understand why you don't want to taste something, and particularly since I always encourage my daughter to taste things, so that she can decide for herself if she likes something or not.

For lunch, I had a filling smoothie and then cycled to the gym to do an hour of exercise.

I wasn't really hungry when I got home, but I was thirsty, so I drank a sauerkraut juice with a spoon of immunil, a kind of honey mixture I eat to feel more energetic.

I was full of energy again, so I started to clean up and organize my home. Just in time too, because afterward, a friend came over, and I made dinner for her. She loved the soup and ate flax-seed crackers with it.

Although I was calmer and my digestive system was quieter, I had a craving to eat something else. In the evening, I felt slightly nauseous. I was freezing and felt hungry. I ended the day with a tablespoon of chia seeds soaked in hot ginger water and one almond, so I wouldn't have to sleep on a starving stomach.

Exercise: Biking for 30 minutes, training with a ball for 45 minutes

5:00 AM $\frac{1}{8}$ cup wheat grass
7:30 AM Fruit porridge
9:30 AM 2 scoops of vanilla Sunwarrior, a cashew, two strawberries
2:00 PM 8 ounces of green broccoli smoothie
5:00 PM 2 cups sauerkraut juice, 5 coconut chips
7:00 PM Green dill soup
10:00 PM 1 tablespoon soaked chia seeds, 1 almond

Day Three

Going through a cleanse and holding a one-day training course in raw food inspiration is difficult. I had to constantly remind myself that I must not eat any of the delicious food I was preparing. I usually don't have the time to sit down and figure out what to eat during this kind of day; instead, I eat something while I'm talking to the course participants. But now, I was mentally prepared and had a plan. I made a little extra of the green smoothies, green soups, and fruit soup samples that the participants were trying, so that I could fill up on those. I also had tiny tastes of the other dishes I prepared, because I needed to know what the food I was offering tasted like.

I felt very refreshed, calm, happy, confident, and curious about the rest of the week. I realized how observant I'd become in noticing how foods affected me. My body really wasn't craving any other types of foods, it just wanted fresh greens.

Exercise: A 40 minute walk

9:00 AM 1 zucchini, 2 apples, cinnamon, combined into a morning porridge
12:00 PM ½ fennel, 1 pear, combined into a morning porridge
2:00 PM a glass of green melon smoothie, 2 cups sauerkraut juice
4:00 PM 3 cups of green soup
8:00 PM Tomato soup with avocado and arugula
10:30 PM 1 scoop of Sunwarrior protein powder

Day Four

I woke up after only five hours of sleep. I felt fresh, rested, calm, and beautiful. I could see everything clearly and I felt confident. It had been only a few days, but I trusted myself to just go with what I felt. I ate more frequently and my portions were smaller, which is something I was comfortable with.

I noticed how I sometimes put something in my mouth, without really feeling what my body wanted. It was becoming clearer to me that eating food can be a way to repress feelings. I felt a bit chilly, but I wasn't tired. The Coldness is an indication that the body is losing weight and cleaning itself. That afternoon, I was feeling too cold and felt my energy decreasing, so I ate a raw tahini ball, which made me feel more balanced.

Training: Bike 30 minutes, TRX 30 minutes (Born in the Navy SEALs, TRX® Suspension Training ® bodyweight exercise simultaneously develops strength, power, endurance, durability, balance, flexibility, and core stability.)

6:30 AM 2 scoops of Sunwarrior protein powder

8:00 AM 1 cup of chia seed porridge in almond milk (left-overs that turned into a take away breakfast, since I left home early in the morning and didn't want the blender to make noise)

10:05 AM 2 cups of green smoothie

12:30 PM 1 tablespoon of green powder, 1 ½ cups green smoothie

3:05 PM 2 cups of sauerkraut juice, 1 tahini ball

5:05 PM 2 cups of green soup with ½ cup algae, 3 tablespoons of coconut chips

7:00 PM 1 tablespoon of chia seeds in tea (1 cup when soaked)

Day Five

I had my first colon cleanse. I'd read a lot about it but never tried it before. When the intestinal cleansing was over, I felt tired, lethargic, and brittle. I felt sad, but calm. I had an avocado soup in the evening, but I felt weird eating after the intestinal cleanse.

6:15 AM 2 scoops of Sunwarrior protein powder
8:15 AM Fruit porridge
11:00 AM 3 cups of green smoothie
12:30 PM 1 tablespoon chia seeds (soaked in ½ cup of tea)
5:00 PM 2 cups of sauerkraut juice
7:00 PM a few pieces of papaya, a taste of Saga's food, 1 ½ cups of green smoothie
9:00 PM 1 avocado

Day Six

I felt like I could eat like this for the rest of my life. This is it! I was noticing how I was starting to get in touch with myself again and trusting my intuition. Although I usually eat mainly raw food and healthy cooked food, I feel that the noise that can appear when you eat too much unhealthy food starts to disappear during a detox. It's like tuning in to your own wavelength or frequency, and you can immediately tell when it's changing. I could fit into a pair of jeans that didn't fit me at the start of the week. I didn't weigh or measure myself before the cleanse, but jeans are always a good measurement. My skin was glowing, soft, and smooth. My eyes were brighter, and I had fresh breath. The cleanse was making me feel and look good. However, I was noticing that I got hungry at night. I found that the best thing to do was to go to bed, so that I didn't start eating things that weren't part of the cleanse.

8:30 AM Fruit porridge

10:00 AM 2 scoops of Sunwarrior protein powder

12:30 PM 3 cups of green smoothie

2:00 PM 2 cups of sauerkraut juice

3:30 PM 1 cup of chia seeds in cinnamon tea, 2 tablespoons of coconut oil with mesquite and carob

6:30 PM 3 cups of green soup

9:00 PM ½ tahini ball, 1 apple

Day Seven

It was a strange day, because we drove to a ski resort in the mountains, but I was prepared. However, my energy was decreasing, and I experienced motion sickness, so I had to eat two raw tahini balls and some coconut flakes. I felt a lot better afterwards. Once we arrived at the ski resort, our daughter Saga hurt herself, and we had to go to the hospital to have her wound stitched. I was trembling from the anxiety, and my dinner was late, so I felt that I needed to calm down. I came close to resorting to food, but instead, I sat down with a cup of tulsi tea (a tea that seems to be calming) to take a moment and just let myself feel whatever it was that I was feeling.

6:30 AM Sunpower protein powder

8:15 AM 2 cups of green smoothie

10:15 AM ⅛ cup of chia seeds in tea, 2 tahini balls

12:00 PM 4 cups of green smoothie

4:00 PM 4 cups of green smoothie

6:00 PM 2 cups of sauerkraut juice plus 2 tablespoons coconut chips

7:30 PM 2 cups of green soup, some coconut chips, a buckwheat crunch, and one tablespoon maca powder

9:00 PM 4 small raw chocolate pieces (in order to not fall asleep when I put my daughter to bed)

In summary, I stuck to the parts of the detox that really worked for me. It's only through our own experiences that we can become wiser and improve ourselves. My husband told me that, after the detox, I was glowing in a new way, and I feel that a change happened within me. I lost weight, my skin was nice and soft, I was in closer contact with myself and my spiritual life. I felt at ease and gained a different appreciation for life.

The cleanse was like an illustration of what I really needed: the courage to be who I am and to love myself. I'm beautiful. I have power.

I also discovered several things that I feel very good about and will continue to do:

- Eat every three hours
- Eat or drink lots of greens
- Drink some of the food that I usually eat
- Avoid eating late at night, to give my body the chance to take a break from digestion. This makes me sleep better, and I wake up feeling more alert and refreshed.

I hope you find my week of green smoothies inspirational; maybe you're ready to give it a try as well?

Tips for those who want to do a cleanse:

- Prepare by having lots of fruits and vegetables at home.
- Plan the number of meals you need to have on hand.
- Drink, and don't forget to chew every three hours, so you don't feel too hungry.
- Drink enough of the green smoothie. (I didn't drink as much as one could; one gallon per day is recommended.)
- If you're feeling cold, it's a sign of cleansing and that you might be consuming fewer calories than what you're used to. You can choose to eat something small, rest, drink soothing herbal tea, put more clothes on, or take a hot bath/shower.
- Focus on giving your cells peace and love.
- Take one day at a time; don't look at your green smoothie week as Mount Everest—a mountain that only a few can climb. One step at a time—one smoothie at a time.
- Find motivation and stick with it.
- Help the intestines to "keep up" by eating flax seed or chia seeds.
- Enhance your smoothie with a vegetable protein powder if you are exercising and need extra food.
- Focus on your successes rather than your failures.
- Be careful in finishing your cleanse. Prepare what you are going to eat after your cleanse is over. Don't just say, "Yay, its over" and eat a pizza. Prepare yourself mentally and plan what you want to eat. Continue drinking your green smoothies and start introducing one meal a day for about a week.

"Smoothies are a great way to use up any leftover veggies or fruits in the kitchen."

"You get all the essential nutrients in one quick shot!"

Bob Dagger cooked raw even as a teenager in the '70s, and he opened America's first raw food store in New York City in 1990. Within a few years, this became his career, replacing his previous jobs as a jeweler, musician, and photographer! However, you can still hear him playing the guitar at the store while chatting with clients between notes!

I started making green smoothies in 1993. This was in the early days of the raw movement, and at that time, we called them blends or raw soups. When I originally started in the raw world, it was just a continuation of my love for fruits and veggies. The idea of a raw movement hadn't really come into consciousness. I was in a relationship at the time, and we became close with another couple (David and Annie Jubb), who wrote one of the first raw recipe books. They were brilliant at creating and explaining the power of healing through food and

Quick fact box:

Name: Robert Andrew Dagger III
a.k.a. "Dagger"
Age: I have stepped out of time
Lives: When you read this I will be somewhere else.
Family: Throw an apple in any schoolyard and you will hit one of my kids
Occupation: Dreamer/entrepreneur/musician/artist/writer/gardener/perpetual five-year-old/www.Highvibe.com and High Vibe retail/wholesale located at 138 East 3rd Street, New York City, NY 10009; 1 (888) 554-6645

cleanses. At that time, I was more focused on art and music, but I was also well-versed in cleanses and healing through food. When I was a teenager, I lived in a teepee for many summers, cooking food and attending workshops by notable authors and lecturers. This is when I started working with what is now called raw foods. For me, it was great working with vegetables and fruits and not having to cook them. I made smoothies for the guests, especially the ones with special requests for vegetarian food; I would bring them my delicious blended soups and fruit smoothies, and they were hooked; and this was in the 1970s!

OK, back to the 1990s—my partner and I, along with David and Annie Jubb, started traveling the country, giving lectures and doing retreats about the virtues of raw foods, fasting, and enjoying "blends." David and Annie also made the best smoothies I had ever tasted! It was a great time, everything was new and there were fewer than twenty books on raw foods and cleansing with raw foods. We were creating what did not exist; man, it was fun!

Throughout our journey, I realized that most people could not get amazing raw food-based supplements, vitamins, and other items. So, I started High Vibe Health and Healing out of a closet in our apartment in New York City. A few years later it replaced my other jobs as a jeweler, musician, and photographer.

By the late '90s, High Vibe Health and Healing was booming, and we moved into my basement art studio on East 3rd Street, next to a notorious motorcycle club's chapter building. We realized early on that we were the first raw store in the States and every day was very exciting; we were making great food and many different smoothies for ourselves and sharing them with our clients. Our clients would get excited and then make them on their own. I also brought together many of those who would become the biggest names in the raw food world, people such as the Boutenkos family, David Wolfe, Jeremy Safron, Douglas Graham, and anyone who would be or was already working in the raw world. They spoke or held workshops during cooking classes at High Vibe. This was where I and all the greatest managers of the 1990s and early 2000s taught others how to make raw foods. My classes were always based on smoothies, as they were my favorites. At this time, there were no raw restaurants and the New York raw movement was just starting. Future restaurateurs and raw food stores were our clients; it was an exciting time.

Back to the food—I think that smoothies are brilliant, and my first recipes were based on Ann Wigmore's. She was a genius and knew how to use smoothies to heal conditions or at least turn them around quickly, though her smoothies tasted horrible. I tweaked her recipes to make them taste amazing. I love the fact that in just one smoothie there are usually more veggies than an average household eats in a week. What a great way to introduce more veggies into your diet and to do so in a way that most people can enjoy. It is an easy and tasty way to get greens into our bodies without having to juice. I love juice, but juicing can be very inefficient, because you are tossing out all the bulk. Creative people back then and to this day use juice leftovers to make delicious dehydrated foods. In my opinion, that is just too much work. I love adding the bulk into the smoothie. For a thicker or thinner consistency you can add more or less water, juice, or coconut water. Each time you create one, it will be amazing. I find smoothies are a great way to use up any leftover veggies or fruits in the kitchen.

Another great thing is that all you need is a blender, which is easier than a juicer to use and to clean. The other thing about blenders is that you do *not* need a high-priced, super-powerful model; with the less powerful ones, you just need to cut the fruits and veggies to a smaller size when creating your smoothie. I believe everything should be simple and balanced. Balance is the key word. Keep everything simple and all will be perfect. Being creative is finding ways to do what you love regardless of any of the obstacles that we perceive are there.

Smoothies are the best way for our bodies and brain to get all the essential nutrients in one quick shot. Smoothies also simplify what our bodies have to do to break down and digest fruits and vegetables. They create very small and multi-surfaced molecules that are able to break down in our bodies without using much energy. By saving energy in digestion, we are able to use this newfound energy to be more vibrant in our daily creative and compassion-generating lives. I see all of you smiling now while drinking a smoothie and reading this beautiful book!

My favorite recipe:

Papaya Sunflower Nectar:
1 papaya medium size
¼ – ½ pound sunflower or any sp
Any green, leafy vegetable you ha
1 tablespoon or so of raw almond butter
1–3 tablespoons coconut butter
Water or coconut water (to fill blender
thinner or thicker to taste)
Avocado (optional)
Add ingredients to blender—blend and
enjoy!

My top tips for green smoothies:

"Papaya or apples make the greens taste
amazing. When having someone try one,
don't say what's in it. Just smile, take a sip,
and say,'Wow, I know you will love this, and
you will feel so beautiful.' That's why I drink
green smoothies! They taste great and of
course they make me feel wonderful."

**The funniest comment someone made
when I talked about green smoothies:**

"Can't remember a funny comment, just
watched people's eyes watching in amaze-
ment."

When do you drink your smoothies?

"The question is when do I not drink
them! OK, I drink them all the time; I have no
exact times."

Green Breakfasts

Green Breakfast is a green smoothie that resembles porridge more than anything. It contains much less water than other smoothies and is served in a bowl. The idea is to eat something light for breakfast, so that the body gets the chance to clear the food you ate the previous day. When we wake up, we're automatically dehydrated and acidic, therefore, we need to start the day by hydrating the body and restoring its pH balance. Feel free to add a powder that will boost your energy (see pages 45–48). If you're extra hungry, top it off with raw granola, raw muesli, hemp seeds, or goji berries. If you want to change a green porridge into a green smoothie, just add some water and serve in a glass.

Green Morning

Green apples aren't as sweet as red apples and will renew your energy.

2 Granny Smith apples, peeled
4 celery stalks
½ inch cucumber
⅛ inch ginger
¼ cup water

Chop the apple, celery stalks, and cucumber into pieces. Peel ginger and cut into pieces. Blend it all with the water. Add more water until desired consistency is reached.

Fennel Breakfast

Fennel for breakfast? When you combine it with red apples, the anise flavor of the fennel emerges and gives a fresh start to the morning.

1 fennel (about 2 cups)
3 red apples
¼ cup of water
Optional: sprinkle hemp seeds and goji berries on top

Cut the fennel and apples into pieces. Blend with a little water until desired consistency is reached. Top with hemp seeds and goji berries.

Smooth Morning

In the morning, we all need to prepare ourselves for what adventures the day may bring. I love feeding my body with a Smooth Morning, which makes me ready to face the challenges and surprises that await. The zucchini adds creaminess to the breakfast porridge and helps to hydrate the body.

2 apples
1 zucchini
water
Optional: crushed flaxseed and cinnamon

Cut the apples and zucchini into pieces. Blend it all with a little water. Top with a little crushed flaxseed and cinnamon.

Green Chia Pudding

Chia seeds stabilize blood sugar, support the stomach, and give you lots of antioxidants and beneficial fatty acids. It's the perfect start for anyone who's usually hungry in the morning.

1 banana
2 apples
3 stalks of celery
2 tablespoons chia seeds, soaked in 1 cup of water, will make about 2 cups of chia porridge
2 teaspoons açaí powder

Mix cut-up pieces of apple and celery with banana, chia seeds, and açaí powder until it turns into a smooth porridge.

Green Smoothies

There are endless varieties of green smoothies. Use the recipes to find your favorites and make up your own combinations. Use the spread on page 34 to get started with your experiments. Good luck!

Grandma Love

Collards such as kale flourish in the winter and provide a great green alternative. This is one of my green winter favorites.

2 cups green kale
2 cups water
1 apple
1 pear
3 dates
1 tablespoon lucuma

Blend the minced green kale with water. Add pieces of the apple and pear and pitted dates and blend again. Add one tablespoon of lúcuma and mix. Add more water until desired consistency is reached.

Asian Green Smoothie

Bok choy is common in the Asian kitchen. Usually steamed or stir-fried, it's also ideal as a green base in a smoothie!

1 cup bok choy
1 cup green beans
1 cup alfalfa sprouts
½–1 tablespoon fresh ginger, peeled
2 cups water
1 tablespoon lime juice
2 pears

Blend the bok choy and pieces of green beans, alfalfa sprouts, and small pieces of peeled ginger with the water. Add lime and pieces of pear. Blend again. Add water until desired consistency is reached.

$2
8oz.
box

Refresh

Grapefruit provides a tangy, slightly bitter taste, which makes for a fresh-tasting smoothie.

2 handfuls of kale
1 ½ cups water
1 grapefruit, peeled and separated into segments
½ avocado

Chop up the kale and mix with water. Add the grapefruit segments and scooped-out avocado and blend again.

Sprout Smoothie

Sprouts contain lots of nutrients and living enzymes, including chlorophyll.
Add them to the other greens to optimize your smoothie.

2 cups spinach
1 cup green lentil sprouts
2 cups water
1 large pear
1 tablespoon of açaí
½ tablespoon of camu camu
1 avocado

Blend spinach and green lentil sprouts with water. Add the chopped pears, açaí, camu camu and mix again. Add the scooped-out avocado. Dilute with water until desired consistency is reached.

Apple Glory

Eating apples every day builds a great foundation for good health. An apple a day keeps the doctor away!

2 apples
2 cups spinach
2 cups water
½ avocado

Chop the apple into pieces and blend it with spinach and water. Mix again. Add water until desired consistency is reached.

GREEN Smoothie Miracle

Green Pear Smoothie

Use ripe pears for a smoother and creamier smoothie.

2 large handfuls of kale
2 cups water
2 large pears, ripe
1 cup blueberries, frozen

Blend chopped kale with the water. Add pieces of pears and blueberries and mix again. Dilute with water for desired consistency.

Daily Green Smoothie

Many of the green smoothies are based on what you have at home. Here is a variation on my "I'll-use-what-I-have-smoothie!"

2 cups mixed salad
2 cups water
½ cup broccoli
½ inch cucumber
1 kiwi
2 pears
½ avocado

Mix the salad with the water. Add pieces of broccoli and cucumber.
Blend. Add pieces of kiwi and pears. Scoop out the avocado and mix into the smoothie. Add more water until desired consistency is reached.

Garden Smoothie

Wild leaves are really the best green leaves that you can use in your smoothie. Miner's lettuce is one of my favorites, and it grows right outside my house. Organic, locally grown, and free!

2 cups miner's lettuce (or other wild green leaves)
1 tablespoon hemp protein powder
1–2 cups water
2 cups honeydew melon

Mix miner's lettuce with hemp seed protein powder and water. Cut honeydew melon into pieces and add to mixture. Add more water until desired consistency is reached.

Fresh!

Serve with ice cubes for a really fresh and delicious smoothie. Mint is also good for digestion.

1 cup mint
1–2 cups water
2 pears
1 tbsp lime juice

Blend chopped mint with one cup of water. Add cut-up pears and lime juice, and mix again. Dilute with more water until desired consistency is reached.

GREEN Smoothie Miracle

Green Lúcuma Smoothie

Lúcuma is a superfood that contains high levels of B3 and iron and gives the smoothie a creamy, caramel flavor.

1 ½ cups lettuce
2 cups water
1 pear
1 apple
1 small zucchini
2 tablespoons lúcuma

Chop the lettuce and mix with water. Cut the pear, apple, and zucchini into pieces and add. Blend again. Add the lúcuma and dilute with water until desired consistency is reached.

Green Smoothie with Chaga Tea

Chaga grows on trees and is super-nutritious and especially rich in antioxidants. It's the perfect base for a green smoothie.

2 cups spinach
2 cups chaga tea
2 celery stalks
½ cucumber
1 apple
⅛ inch ginger, peeled
1 avocado

Blend spinach with chaga tea. Cut celery, cucumber, ginger, and apple into pieces. Add the ingredients to the blender and mix. Scoop out the avocado and add more water until desired consistency is reached.

Sea-buckthorn Smoothie

Sea-buckthorn can be purchased fresh or frozen. It's rich in vitamin C and antioxidants, which make your skin glow.

1 cup lettuce
1 cup sunflower shoots
1 cup sea-buckthorn
2 cups water

Mix all the ingredients with water. Add more water until desired consistency is reached.

Strawberrylicious

Fresh and cool strawberry smoothie! Basil and strawberries are both rich in iron.

2 cups strawberries
2 cups basil
1 tablespoon lime juice
1 cup water
½ cup ice cubes
Optional; honey to sweeten

Mix strawberries, basil, lime juice, and water. Add ice cubes and mix again.

Green Orange

Spruce up your traditional orange juice with spinach. Kids love it!

2 cups orange juice
2 cups spinach

Blend the ingredients and enjoy!

Iron Smoothie

Parsley contains lots of iron, which is especially good for women.

2 cups flat-leaf parsley
2 cups water
2 apples
1 zucchini
1 tbsp lemon juice

Mix parsley with water. Cut apples and zucchini into pieces. Add remaining ingredients and blend again. Dilute with more water until desired consistency is reached.

Green Kiwi Smoothie

Kiwi is a fruit that isn't too sweet and gives the smoothie a tart, fresh taste reminiscent of yogurt.

6 inch cucumber
1 kiwi
2 cups lettuce
1 tablespoon lemon juice
1 avocado

1 tbsp lemon juice
1–2 cups of water

Cut the cucumber and kiwi into chunks. Mix together with lettuce, scooped-out avocado, lemon juice, and water. Dilute with water until desired consistency is reached.

Apricot & Melon Smoothie

This is a real summer smoothie with melon and fresh orange apricots. It's spiked with the power of sunflower shoots and spinach, and it's also hydrating because of the cucumber and water. Bring it in a thermos to the beach!

2 cups melon
4 inches cucumber
1 cup apricot
1 cup spinach
1 cup sunflower shoots
2 cups water

Cut the melon, cucumber, and apricots into chunks. Mix with spinach, sunflower shoots, and water. Dilute with water until desired consistency is reached.

CHEW YOUR SMOOTHIE WITH LOVE

- Customize recipes and portion sizes according to how much you need to drink in order to feel full.
- Add water to achieve your preferable consistency. You might like a texture that's more liquid or creamier. You might even want to eat your smoothie with a spoon. My advice is that you familiarize yourself with the green smoothies and adjust water according to the amount you like the best.
- Portions vary, depending on whether you're a slender woman or a big guy.
- The portions of the recipes are estimated to serve two people, unless otherwise noted.

TIP! If you like cold smoothies, add a few ice cubes.

Green Passion

Passion fruit gives this smoothie a tart flavor, and the creaminess derives from the banana . . . Exotic!

1 cup spinach
2 cups water
3 passion fruits
2 bananas

Blend the spinach with water. Scoop out the pulp from the passion fruit and add together with peeled and sliced bananas. Mix. Add more water until desired consistency is reached.

Green Broccoli Smoothie

Broccoli contains more starch than green leaves, which makes for a more filling smoothie!

1 cup broccoli
2 pears
1 cup spinach
1 cup sunflower shoots
3 tablespoons lemon juice
3 cups water

Cut the brocoli and pear into pieces. Mix with spinach, sunflower shoots, lemon juice and water. Dilute with more water until desired consistency is reached.

Apple Green

Arugula has a spicy taste and adds a peppery flavor to the smoothie.
The bitterness of the arugula promotes digestion.

2 handfuls of arugula
1–2 cups water
2 apples, red
⅛ inch cucumber
1 teaspoon lemon juice
½ avocado

Blend arugula with 1 cup of water. Cut the apple and cucumber into pieces. Add the remaining ingredients, except for the avocado, and blend again. Add the scooped-out avocado and mix, dilute with water until desired consistency is reached.

Pomegreen Smoothie

Tip! To pick out the small red pomegranate seeds, cut the fruit in half, gently squeeze the skin, and turn it inside out over a bowl. Remove the seeds. Discard the white parts of the skin, which can taste bitter. Strain the juice, pour into a beautiful glass, and add the kernels to the smoothie.

2 cups salad
1–2 cups water
2 pears
1 cup (about ½ pomegranate) pomegranate kernels.

Blend the salad with 1 cup of water. Cut the pear into pieces and add the other ingredients before mixing again. Add more water until desired consistency is reached.

Green Grape Smoothie

Whenever you buy grapes, you should look for organic ones with seeds.

2 cups crisp lettuce
2 cups water
2 cups greens grapes with seeds
1 pear

Blend the crispy salad with water. Seed grapes and cut the pear into pieces. Add the remaining ingredients and blend again. Dilute with more water until desired consistency is reached.

Apple Pie Smoothie

With a little imagination, this smoothie resembles a scrumptious apple pie!

2 handfuls of spinach
1–2 cups water
2 red apples
2 tablespoon lúcuma powder
1–2 teaspoons cinnamon

Blend the spinach with 1 cup of water. Cut the apple into pieces. Add the remaining ingredients and mix again. Dilute with water until desired consistency is reached.

Green Christmas Smoothie

Sharon is a typical Christmas fruit. Don't worry if the fruit has some brown spots, as it's just a little sugar that has precipitated in the skin.

2 handfuls of kale
2–3 cups of water
1 large persimmon or two sharon fruit
1–2 teaspoons cinnamon

Chop kale and mix with 1 cup of water. Cut persimmons/sharon into pieces and add together with cinnamon. Mix again. Add water until desired consistency is reached.

Papaya with Lime Smoothie

Papaya contains an extremely beneficial enzyme that helps our digestive system.

2 handfuls of spinach
1–2 cups water
¼ large papaya
½ lime juice

Blend the spinach and 1 cup of water. Add chunks of papaya and lime juice and mix again. Add water until desired consistency is reached.

Ginger Green Smoothie

2 handfuls of kale
2 cups water
6 soaked figs, 2–4 hours
½ inch ginger

Chop the kale and mix with 1 cup of water. Add figs and peeled, chopped ginger and blend again. Add water until desired consistency is reached.

GREEN Smoothie

Green Creamy Apricot Smoothie

Dried apricots should be brown. Avoid buying the orange ones, which are sulfurized, meaning that sulfur has been added. This is done to inhibit bacteria and fungi and to preserve the color. However, this can also cause asthma.

1 cup nettle
1 cup spinach
½ cup of soaking water
1 ½ cup water
1 red apple
8 soaked apricots, soaked 2–4 hours

Chop the nettles and mix with spinach, water, and the water from the apricots. Add pieces of apples and apricots, and mix again.

Cacao Dessert Smoothie

A smoothie that's lunch and dessert in one!

2 handfuls of kale
2 cups water
2 dates
2 tablespoons raw cacaopowder
1 tablespoon honey
1 avocado

Chop the kale and mix with the water. Add the pitted dates, cocoa, and honey and blend again. Add scooped-out avocado and more water until desired consistency is reached.

Evening Glory

In the jungle of the night, a green smoothie can increase your strength and make you glow against the dark sky.

2 cups spinach
2 cups water
1 pear
½ cucumber
½ lime juice
½ avocado

Mix the spinach with water. Add chunks of pears and cucumber as well as lime juice. Blend again. Mix in the scooped-out avocado. Add water until desired consistency is reached.

Raspberry Meets Mesquite

Mesquite has a taste that's reminiscent of maple syrup but a little smokier. I like to call the flavor smoky sweet!

2 handfuls of spinach
2 cups water
¾ cups raspberries, thawed
2 tablespoons mesquite
2 tablespoons honey
½ avocado

Mix spinach with water. Add the remaining ingredients, except for the avocado, and mix. Finally, add the scooped-out avocado and dilute with water until desired consistency is reached.

Blackcurrant Smoothie

Blackcurrant is a berry with a very low glycemic index, and during spring and summer you can substitute them for the spinach.

2 handfuls of spinach
2 cups water
½ cup thawed blackcurrants
4 soaked apricots, 2–4 hours
½ avocado

Mix the spinach with water. Add blackcurrants and apricots and blend again. Mix in the avocado. Add water until desired consistency is reached.

Immune Booster Smoothie

A little fresh ginger in a green smoothie will boost your immune system, and the açaí powder contains lots of antioxidants, healthy fatty acids, and protein.

2 cups of spinach
2 cups water
⅛ inch fresh ginger
1 pear
4 soaked figs, 2–4 hours
1 tablespoon açaí powder

Mix spinach with the water. Peel the ginger and cut into pieces along with the pears. Add remaining ingredients and blend again. Dilute with more water until desired consistency is reached.

Saga's Green Melon Smoothie

My daughter was once drinking this smoothie and exclaimed, "Mom, you'll have to make this for me often!" Serve with ice cubes on a hot day.

10–20 mint leaves
⅕ cup water
1 cucumber, peeled
½ honeydew melon
1 tablespoon honey, optional

Blend the mint with water. Cut the cucumber and melon into pieces. Add remaining ingredients and mix again.

Strong & Green

Green smoothies are perfect both before and after exercise. Celery and green leaves make your bones strong, hemp protein makes your muscles grow, and the lemon makes the body alkaline.

2 cups red leaf lettuce
2 cups water
2 celery stalks
1 pear (ripe)
3 tablespoons hemp protein powder
2 tablespoons lemon juice
1 avocado

Mix the red leaf lettuce with the water. Cut celery and pears into pieces. Add hemp protein powder and lemon juice. Blend again. Scoop out the avocado and mix into the smoothie.

Wasabi Smoothie

You normally eat wasabi with sushi, but in this case, it adds a little extra heat to the smoothie. If you don't have wasabi paste, use wasabi powder and adjust the amount according to taste.

4 celery stalks
1 cucumber, peeled
$\frac{1}{5}$ cup water
$\frac{1}{10}$ inch wasabi paste
2 tablespoons honey

Chop celery and cucumber into pieces. Blend with the water. Add remaining ingredients and mix again.

Basil - Purple

Excellent for garnishes and salads. Widely used for flavored vinegar, giving the vinegar a wine color.

FULL SUN   ANNUAL

GREEN Smoothie Mix

Green x3 Smoothie

Green from green leaves, green from the algae spirulina, and green from wheat grass powder—it doesn't get any better than this.

1 cup spinach
2 cups water
1 cup pineapple
1 cup mango
1 teaspoon lemon
1 teaspoon spirulina
2 teaspoons wheat grass powder

Mix spinach and the water. Peel the pineapple and mango and cut into chunks. Add remaining ingredients and blend again.

RED
SWEET CHARD
99¢
LB

BOSTON
LETTUCE
$1.49
EA

Green soups

Green soups are a more filling version of green smoothies. They're perfect as a light lunch on the go or a late dinner at home. The body doesn't need as much food in the evening, which makes green soup the perfect food if you're eating dinner late. When I eat green soups for dinner, I like to set the table nicely, pour the soup into a beautiful bowl, and really enjoy my meal in peace and quiet.

Red Green Soup

Tart red apples with an earthy beetroot flavor—delicious with greens!

1 cup spinach
1 cup arugula
1–2 cups water
2 red apples
3 sun-dried tomatoes, in oil or soaked
1 cup beetroot
1 avocado

Soak the sun-dried tomatoes for about 1 hour, if you aren't using the ones packed in oil. Add spinach and arugula with 1 cup of water to the blender. Mix. Add apple slices, sun-dried tomatoes, and peeled pieces of beets, and mix again. Add scooped-out avocado, dilute with more water, and blend again. Add more water until desired consistency is reached.

Green Beetroot Soup with Salty Capers and Spicy Mustard

Beetroot and Dijon mustard is the perfect combination. Add capers and you have a delicious soup.

2 cups of spinach
1–2 cups water
5 sun-dried tomatoes, soak for one hour if you're using the dried ones that are not packed in oil in a jar
1 cup beetroot
3–4 teaspoons Dijon mustard
1 avocado
2 tablespoons capers

Soak the sun-dried tomatoes for about one hour. Add spinach and 1 cup of water in the blender and mix. Add sun-dried tomatoes, peeled pieces of beets, and mustard, and mix again. Add scooped-out avocado and blend again. Dilute with more water until desired consistency is reached.

Green Miso Soup

If it's cold outside, but you still want to enjoy a green soup, use lukewarm miso as a base instead of water.

2 cups water
2 tablespoons miso
2 cups of spinach
6 sun-dried tomatoes, soak for one hour if you're using the dried ones that are not packed in oil in a jar
½ tablespoon lime juice
1 avocado

Heat water to room temperature. Mix water, miso, and spinach. Add sun-dried tomatoes and lime juice and mix again. Add scooped-out avocado and blend.

Green Curry Soup

Broccoli doesn't belong in the green leaves category, but it's still rich in chlorophyll.

1 cup broccoli
2 red apples
1 ½ cups water
1 avocado
Any kind of curry

Cut the broccoli and apples into pieces. Blend with the water. Add scooped-out avocado and mix again. Dilute with more water until desired consistency is reached. Dust with ground curry before serving.

GREEN Smoothie Miracle

Green Soup with Indian Spices

Indian spices warm you up from the inside, and the turmeric helps to keep the joints flexible.

1 cup watercress
2 cups of spinach
1–2 cups water
2 inches ginger
1–2 tablespoons lime juice
⅛ teaspoon turmeric
½ teaspoon cumin
1 avocado

Mix spinach and watercress with 1 cup of water. Add peeled pieces of ginger, turmeric, cumin, and lime juice, and mix again. Add scooped-out avocado and blend again. Add more water until desired consistency is reached.

Parsley Love

Parsley is one of my absolute favorites as a base for salads and smoothies; it's green, crispy, and loaded with iron.

About 1 cup leaf parsley
1 cup water
7 sun-dried tomatoes, soaked for 30 minutes
3 tomatoes
2 inches leek
2 teaspoons lemon juice
1 teaspoon salt (optional)

Chop the parsley into small pieces. Mix parsley and water. Add chunks of sun-dried tomatoes, tomatoes, and leek, as well as lemon juice. Blend again. Add a little salt. Add more water until desired consistency is reached.

Green Gazpacho

Serve with ice cubes on a hot summer day. You can prepare it in advance and store it in the freezer. Let it thaw for about 30 minutes before serving

1 cup arugula
1–2 cups water
1 green bell pepper
1 ½ yellow onion (soak in water for 30 minutes to prevent a bitter flavor)
1 small cucumber
4 tomatoes
3 celery stalks
4 sun-dried tomatoes, soaked for 30 minutes.
Optional: garlic

Mix arugula together with 1 cup water. Add chopped bell peppers, peeled yellow onion, cucumber, tomatoes, and celery, as well as sun-dried tomatoes. Mix again. Add more water until desired consistency is reached.

Green Pea Chilled Soup

Eat it cool on a hot summer day!

1 cup of spinach
2 ½ cups water
½ a pear
1 cup green peas, frozen
1 avocado

Mix the spinach with 1 cup of water. Add the chopped up pears and green peas. Add scooped-out avocado and blend again. Dilute with water until desired consistency is reached.

Green Virgin Mary Soup

Green leaves on the celery can be added to the soup to make it greener.

4 celery stalks, preferably with leaves
1 inch of fresh red chili
1–2 cups water
3 ½ cups (50 ml) tomato juice
2 tablespoons honey
1 pinch of black pepper
Serve with: celery stalk and black pepper

Chop the celery and chili. Mix with water. Add tomato juice, honey, and black pepper. Blend again. Add more water until desired consistency is reached. Top with a couple of sliced celery stalks and black pepper.

Tummy Booster Soup

Sauerkraut is fermented cabbage. This increases the nutritional content. The fermentation process also creates bacteria that our stomach loves and wants every day.

2 cups of spinach
½ cup parsley
3 cups water
1 ½ avocado
Optional: tamari and a pinch of salt if needed.
Topping: 2 tablespoons sauerkraut plus 1 tablespoon parley per serving

Mix the spinach, chopped parsley, and water. Add the scooped-out avocado and blend again. Add a little salt or tamari, if needed. Top with 2 tablespoons of sauerkraut and 1 tablespoon of parsley, per serving.

Big City Soup

Cilantro is an herb that helps the body clear out heavy metals, which are commonly found in big cities. It's a soup that will help you enjoy a glorious Big City life.

2 cup fresh cilantro
2 cups water
2 avocados
1–2 tablespoons lime juice

Chop the cilantro into smaller pieces and mix with the water. Scoop out the avocadoes and add to the blender with a little lime juice. Mix again. Add more water until desired consistency is reached.

Sweet Pea Shoots

...h in Chlorophyll, Vitamins A and E.

-grown for extra minerals.

...tor. Fresh for one week.

...unchy. Mix with

Sunflower Soup

Sunflower shoots are a great source of both enzymes and chlorophyll. For variation, use pea shoots (see picture).

2 cups salad
1–2 cups of water
1 cup sunflower shoots
2 tablespoons lime juice
1 avocado

Mix water, lettuce and sunflower sprouts. Add the lime juice and avocado and blend again. Add more water until desired consistency is reached.

Oregano Soup

Fresh herbs in a soup or a smoothie enhance the flavor and add lots of goodness.

4 tomatoes
1 cup arugula
1 cup oregano
1 cup basil
1 tablespoon lemon juice
1 avocado

Mix tomatoes until they acquire a liquid consistency. Add the arugula, oregano, basil, and lemon juice, and blend again. Add avocado; blend again. Dilute with water until desired consistency is reached.

Green Dill Soup

You can make this fresh soup extra cool by adding a few ice cubes.

2 cucumbers
1–2 cups of water
1 cup dill
1 cup cilantro
½ tablespoon lemon juice
1 avocado

Cut the cucumber into pieces. Mix cucumber and water. Add the cilantro, dill, and lemon juice. Add avocado and blend again. Dilute with water until desired consistency is reached.

Green Smoothie Milkshakes

Green smoothie milkshakes are ideal for anyone new to green smoothies. They're perfect as a yummy dessert or a delicious snack. These smoothies are often a favorite with children, due to the fact that they're pretty sweet. Green "milkshakes" should be consumed directly after preparation and cannot be saved. Sometimes, I'm a bit mischievous and start the day with a green milk-shake. That's what I call everyday luxury!

Purple Smoothie

Like a purple dream, except it's real.

1 cup spinach
1 cup water
1 cup of blueberries, frozen
1 tablespoon açaí powder
2 frozen bananas

Mix spinach with the water. Add remaining ingredients and mix again.

Tip! Always keep frozen bananas in your freezer, so you are able to make a green smoothie milkshake at any time. Peel the banana, preferably one that's been lying out for a few days; cut the banana into smaller pieces, and store the pieces in a bag in the freezer.

Tip! If you use less water, you can simply transform a green smoothie milkshake into a green ice cream instead!

Blackberry Milkshake

Fill your freezer with frozen berries. The bananas can be frozen or fresh, regardless of the berries.

1 large handful of spinach
1 ½ cups water
½ cup blackberries
2 bananas, frozen or fresh

Mix spinach with the water. Add remaining ingredients and mix.

Mango Sweet

A ripe mango feels soft but not mushy. Cut the mango lengthwise along the pit, slice the flesh in a check pattern down to the skin, turn it inside out, and you'll end up with mango cubes.

2 cups of kale
2 cups water
1 cup of mango, frozen
Optional: 1–2 bananas, frozen

Cut the kale into pieces and mix with water. Add mango and the banana (if desired), and mix again.

Cool Goji Smoothie

Goji berries give your smoothie an orange color because they contain beta-carotene, the same substance that gives carrots their orange color.

2 handfuls of spinach
2 cups water
1/3 cup soaked goji berries, about 1 hour
2 cups frozen cantaloupe

Cut the melon into chunks. Freeze for eight hours. Mix spinach with the water. Add remaining ingredients and blend.

Smoothie Miracle

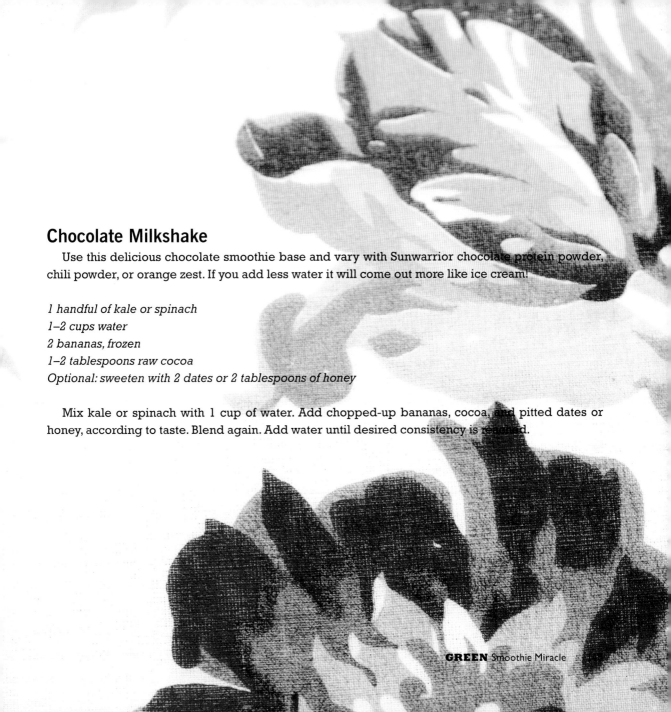

Chocolate Milkshake

Use this delicious chocolate smoothie base and vary with Sunwarrior chocolate protein powder, chili powder, or orange zest. If you add less water it will come out more like ice cream!

1 handful of kale or spinach
1–2 cups water
2 bananas, frozen
1–2 tablespoons raw cocoa
Optional: sweeten with 2 dates or 2 tablespoons of honey

Mix kale or spinach with 1 cup of water. Add chopped-up bananas, cocoa, and pitted dates or honey, according to taste. Blend again. Add water until desired consistency is reached.

Green Likes Strawberries

Strawberries give a taste of summer; add frozen bananas for a creamy strawberry ice cream drink.

1 cup spinach
1 cup water
2 frozen bananas
1 cup of strawberries
Optional: sweeten with 2 tablespoons honey or 2 teaspoons dates

Mix spinach with the water. Add pieces of bananas, strawberries, and honey or pitted dates, if desired. Blend again.

Green Creamy Vanilla Smoothie

Vanilla and frozen bananas—it tastes like real vanilla ice cream!

2 cups of spinach
2 cups water
2 frozen bananas
1 scoop of Sunwarrior vanilla protein powder
Pinch of vanilla powder

Mix spinach with the water. Add chopped bananas and remaining ingredients. Blend again.

Green Mint & Watermelon Sorbet

You can divide a large watermelon into pieces and freeze what you don't eat. Super delicious to add to smoothies for an ice cream sensation!

¾ cup fresh mint
⅓ cups water
3 cups of watermelon, frozen or fresh with ice cubes

Mix mint with the water. Add chunks of watermelon; you can also add some ice cubes. Mix.

Pineapple Sorbet

Use as little water as possible to give this smoothie a consistency similar to sorbet.

1 cup spinach
1 cup water
2 cups pineapple, frozen (in cubes)

Mix spinach with water. Add pineapple and mix again.

Creamy Pineapple Sorbet

With the banana added, this smoothie is perfect for children or anyone who likes a smoothie that's a little sweeter and creamier.

1 cup spinach
1 cup water
½ cup pineapple, frozen
2 bananas, frozen

Mix spinach with the water. Add the remaining chopped ingredients and blend again.

Green Juices

I alternate my green smoothies with heavenly juices. As I explained in the juice chapter on pages 37 and 38, the difference between a green smoothie and a juice is that juices take a short cut past the digestive system. Because there are no fibers, the nutrition goes straight to the blood, cells, and tissues in the body. Juice is broken down and is absorbed within 10–15 minutes, whereas food takes 3–5 hours to be broken down and converted to nutrition. Fiber has no direct nutritional value in the body, but it is important for the functioning of the gut.

Juices build and regenerate the body. They contain all the amino acids, minerals, salts, enzymes, and vitamins the body needs. That is, if the juice is organic, fresh, and has been extracted correctly.

Wheat grass, sprouts, and other green lettuce leaves require a strong juicer; read more under FAQ. When I drink concentrated juice, I dilute it with 25–50 percent pure water.

Totally Green Juice

Cucumber is composed mostly of water that contains minerals, which helps our hair to shine and our nails to stay strong.

1 bunch of celery
1 cucumber
Juice from 1 lemon
2 inches ginger

Sprout Juice

To juice sprouts is to squeeze the best parts out of them. Green lentil sprouts are sweet and quick to sprout at home.

2 cups green lentil sprouts
3 red apples
2 zucchinis

Orange Red Juice

When you juice carrots and beets, you should take advantage of the green foliage, where a lot of chlorophyll is stored. If you want, you can save the foliage and use it as a green base for smoothies. The combination of beets and carrots helps to stimulate the production of blood cells.

10 carrots
3 oranges
7 beetroots
Optional: beet and carrot tops

C-Juice

Carrot and cabbage with lemon and ginger is the perfect combination.

10 carrots
1 cabbage head
1 lemon
⅛ inch ginger

Apple Juice with a Twist

When zucchini is in season, make sure to consume the vegetable in your juices.

4 zucchinis
2 apples
1 lemon

Fennel Juice

Fruit and vegetables often resemble the parts of the body that they serve. Fennel resembles the heart and helps to purify the blood.

2 fennel bulbs
6 pears

Celery Green

Celery helps you to cool off on hot days, because it's rich in sodium.

1 bunch of celery
1 zucchini
1 green apple
1 lime
1 large watermelon

Also use the rind of the watermelon, if it is organic. It contains chlorophyll!

Sauerkraut Juice

2 cups cabbage
1–2 cloves of garlic
Water, enough to cover

Finely grate the cabbage and crush one to two garlic cloves. Put in a glass jar and add enough cold water to cover it. Put the lid on and let stand at room temperature for three days. Pour 1 cup of the slightly tart beverage and drink.

The beverage is loaded with healthy lactic bacteria! Add more water and the cabbage and garlic can be used several times until the flavor becomes unsavory. If you always have two jars of cabbage ready, you'll always have access to lactic bacteria.

Green Wheat Grass —An Energy Boost

Wheat Grass Juice

2 cups wheat grass
1 green apple
1 lemon

Dr. Ann Wigmore healed herself of colon cancer with the help of wheat grass, and with the help of her medical practices, she revolutionized the world. Wheat grass juice is the green juice pressed from wheat grass and is consumed immediately after its extraction. You can grow wheat grass at home, buy it fresh, have a shot of it at the farmers' market, buy it frozen, or use it in the form of powder.

The following points about wheat grass were compiled by Dr. G P Earp-Thomas of Bloomfield Laboratories, who, in collaboration with Dr. Ann Wigmore, has researched the health effects of wheat grass juice and how it can be used as a natural remedy for certain illnesses.

Facts about wheat grass:

1. Wheat grass juice purifies the blood.
2. Wheat grass juice acts as a detergent in the body.
3. Use wheat grass juice as a shampoo to get rid of dandruff. Rub the juice in the scalp, and rinse.
4. Wheat grass used in small amounts in your diet prevents dental cavities.
5. Gargle with wheat grass juice for toothache.
6. Gargle with wheat grass juice for a sore throat
7. Pustules in the mouth. Use wheat grass soaked in juice and place on the damaged area, or chew wheatgrass to heal the pain.
8. Drink wheat grass juice for skin problems.
9. Wheat grass juice prevents hair from turning gray.
10. Use wheat grass juice as a vitamin drink.
11. Use wheat grass to protect and heal skin burn.
12. Wheat grass juice provides a feeling of strength, both in body and in mind, health, patience, and well-being.
13. Wheat grass juice results in cleaner blood and good digestion.
14. Wheat grass juice is an excellent mouthwash that will kill toxins in the gums.
15. Wheat grass juice is great for all kinds of blood diseases, including anemia.
16. Wheat grass juice contains large quantities of enzymes. Enzymes are vital substances. Read more about living enzymes on page 14.
17. Wheat grass juice is an excellent skin cleanser, which can be absorbed through the skin and provide your body with nourishment. Pour the wheat grass juice into a tub of warm water, wash well with wheat grass water for 15–20 minutes, and rinse off in a cold shower.
18. Wheat grass implants or enemas heal and detoxify the colon and other internal organs. First, a normal irrigation is performed; then the wheat grass is implanted—that is to say, at least 3–4 ounces of wheat grass juice are introduced into the intestine and held there for twenty minutes.

19. Wheat grass juice is great for constipation, as it opens the bowels.
20. Wheat grass juice disinfects by removing and killing bacteria.
21. The scientist Dr. Maximilian Bircher-Benner called chlorophyll "concentrated solar power." He believes that chlorophyll improves heart function and affects the cardiovascular system, uterus, intestines, and lungs.
22. According to Dr. Birscher, nature uses chlorophyll as a way to cleanse, rebuild, and neutralize toxins in the body.
23. Wheat grass juice reduces high blood pressure because it reduces the amount of toxins in the body and brings iron to the blood, which improves blood circulation.
24. Wheat grass juice dilates the capillaries (the body's smallest blood vessels).
25. Wheat grass overcomes radiation, decay, and odors in the home.
26. Wheat grass converts hazardous non-organic chemicals into harmless ones. You can add wheat grass to the water in which you rinse pesticide-contaminated fruits and vegetables.
27. Heavy metals such as lead, cadmium, mercury, aluminum, and an excessive amount of copper can successfully be reduced by adding small amounts of wheat grass juice and gradually increasing the amount.
28. Wheat grass is one of the richest sources of natural vitamins A and C. It is also unusually rich in vitamin B. It's an excellent source of calcium, iron, magnesium, phosphorus, potassium, sodium, sulfur, cobalt, zinc, and proteins.
29. Agricultural researcher and German Scientist, Ehrenfried Pfeiffer, states that dried wheat grass contains 47.4 percent protein.
30. Pets can drink wheat grass juice for improved health.

FAQ

Is it expensive to eat smoothies?

If you're replacing a restaurant lunch with a green smoothie, you'll have money left over in the wallet. However, if you're used to eating a packet of noodles or a burger, it can be more expensive. To get the most value for your money, make your green smoothies at home and take them with you.

How do I get started?

Make the decision to replace one meal a day with a smoothie, or try a one- to three-day cleanse. Think green leaves and fruit as a base, and use your own creativity by inventing your own favorite blends. See the table on page 34 for inspiration on making your own recipes.

Who can eat green smoothies?

Young or old, anyone can drink the green smoothies. It's about finding what makes you feel comfortable drinking the smoothies. Babies under one year should avoid spinach and honey. For young children, green smoothies are the healthiest start-up food they can get. Teenagers need all the extra nutrients that the green smoothies provide. In middle age, when we have an active working life, the green smoothie is an easy and filling meal on the go. When we are old and the teeth are fragile, green smoothies are a perfect way of getting nutrients.

Can I work out and drink green smoothies?

Green smoothies provide you with great strength before a workout and restore energy afterwards. When you exercise, an excess of acid can accumulate in your body and make you acidic. When you're acidic, your body takes longer time to recover, which means that you can't exercise as often and as intensely. The green leaves help to make the body more alkaline, which means that you can improve your training results.

Where do I get protein, carbs, and fat?

In order to build muscles and repair tissue, protein is needed. Indeed, every cell in the body contains some form of protein. You might know someone who exercises with weights and eats a lot of animal protein. Maybe you've detected an almost sour smell coming off that person. That's a sign of acidity. The protein in green leaves is of a high quality and is easier for the body to absorb than animal protein, and this causes the body to become more alkaline. It's about quality, not quantity.

Green leaves contain complex carbohydrates. Your brain makes up two percent of your body volume, but uses 20 percent of all your carbohydrates. Carbohydrates are the brain's fuel. When you provide your body with slow carbohydrates, your blood sugar stays stable and your body and mind have a more balanced activity. You can choose between eating a fruit such as a banana, which offers a lot of simple carbohydrates, or a fruit with a lower glycemic index, such as an apple. If you choose to eat only green vegetables, you will get fewer simple carbs.

Green smoothies are not very rich in fat. To maximize your fat intake, you can add avocado, which is a fatty fruit, or cold-pressed oils. Fat is necessary in order to produce cell membranes and for transporting and absorbing fat-soluble vitamins. In addition, we need fat to keep our skin youthful and to prevent desiccation. But remember, adding fat to the smoothie will slow down the absorption of the nutrients in the body, and the drink will be digested at a slower pace.

Can I drink green smoothies if I'm pregnant?

The folic acid found in green leaves is very important to consume before you become pregnant and also during pregnancy. Make sure to buy organic green leaves and rinse them thoroughly. The fiber in green leaves also helps to keep your stomach functioning properly, which is important during pregnancy. Remember that when you're pregnant, the child will take everything it needs and leave you with the leftovers, so load up with enough nutrition for the both of you. Use parsley and super-foods, such as goji berries and açaí powder, which are rich in iron. It's important for a pregnant woman to consume enough iron for her *and* her unborn baby.

How much should I consume if I'm on a green smoothie detox?

If you're only consuming green smoothies, you should drink about 4 quarts a day, spread over five occasions. But remember to vary the amount according to your body size. You shouldn't feel too hungry during a detox. Remember to differentiate between feeling peckish and feeling hungry!

How and for how long do I store my smoothies?

Store your green smoothies in an airtight container, preferably glass, in your refrigerator. Take the beverage out of the fridge about one hour before consumption; it will taste better at room temperature. Smoothies containing frozen bananas or other frozen fruits (except berries) should be consumed immediately. I keep my smoothies for a maximum of one day. To make it easier, I like to mix my morning smoothie in the evening if I know I'm getting up early the next day.

What kind of blender or juicer do I need?

A high-speed blender will allow the beverage to retain more nutrients, compared to using a standard blender. Vitamixer or Blendtec are two good options.

If you're going to squeeze your own green juices, you will need a juice extractor or a juicer. There are a lot of different devices for juice extraction. What you should keep in mind is that the more efficiently the juice has been separated from its fiber, the more nutrients are retained in the juice. The brand Green Star has the ability to maximize derived nutrients.

The most important part is that it fits your wallet and lifestyle!

Can I include my green smoothies in my ordinary diet?

By starting to add green smoothies to your ordinary diet, you will spontaneously start using less salt and sugar, and your body will crave more greens. One green smoothie per day will affect the rest of your meals.

A little about salt: Most of us consume too much salt. We need sodium because it regulates fluid pressure and pH balance. However, all the salt we need can be found in almost all foods.

Too much salt results in a deficiency in potassium and makes our bodies collect fluids.

What is the Glycemic Index?

The GI is a way of measuring how various food substances affect glycemic control. The GI value of different foods is the basis for dietary recommendations in certain diets. The type and the quantity of carbohydrates are the primary compounds that affect the GI value of food. Foods that are high in GI are called "simple carbs," while those with a low glycemic index are called "complex carbs." GI doesn't account for the amount of sugar found in foods, and sugar is the real simple carb.

GREEN Smoothie

Inspiration

Eating for Beauty; David Wolfe, North Atlantic Books, Berkeley, California, 2007/2009
Green For Life; Victoria Boutenko, Raw Family Publishing, Canada, 2005
Green Smoothie Revolution; Victoria Boutenko, North Atlantic Books, Berkeley, California, 2009
Rainbow Green Live-Food Cuisine; Gabriel Cousens, North Atlantic Books, 2003
The Natural Way to Vibrant Health; Dr. N. W. Walker, Norwalk Press, 2008
The Sunfood Diet Success System; David Wolfe, Maul Brothers Publishing, 2006
The pH Miracle; Dr. Robert Young, Warner Books, 2002

Websites:

www.thegardendiet.com
www.terawarner.com
www.sergeiboutenko.com—great for wild edibles
www.highvibe.com

For further inspiration, please consult other books written by Erica Palmcrantz Aziz, published by Skyhorse Publishing, New York; *Raw food—A Complete Guide For Every Meal of the Day, Raw Desserts,* and *Fabulous Raw Food: A Healthier, Simpler Life in Three Weeks.*

Index

Epilogue

Every evening, I read my daughter fairy tales from a very beautiful and well-written children's book, and every night, we make up our own version of the story together. This is one of our stories:

Once there was a girl named Life, who lived in a water droplet in a lake. The lake had been acidified and littered, and the water was no longer clear and healthy. Life and her friend the frog were left at the lake, the birds had flown away and the fish in the water were all sick. One day, Life heard three children walking near the lake and tried to shout for help in her loudest voice. The children heard a faint cry and wondered where it came from. Life's friend the frog blew on the water drop, so that Life could get closer to the children. The more her friend frog blew on her, the bigger she became. The children saw the water droplet with the nice girl inside and stopped.

"Thank you for seeing me," said Life. "You have to help me. My friend the frog and everyone here is feeling very sick."

"Who are you?" the children asked.

"I am Life, the water here, or part of it at least. I have to stay fresh and clean so that the animals and plants are able to live comfortably, but now my friend the frog is sick from all the dirt found in this lake, and he can't live here anymore."

"How can we help you?" asked the children.

Life told the children of a dark force that litters and makes the water unhealthy, so it is impossible for the fish to live in the water and the birds to fly in in the sky. She showed the children how the leaves on the trees had turned brown and the bark was loose around the trunk, and she explained how the trees soaked up the dirty water. She burst into tears and then gave her new friends a pleading look. "Everything that grows and lives is in need of clean air and clean water," she said, "but we believe there is invisible dirt in the air and in the water. "

"We must try to find out where the dark force is coming from and who spreads the visible and invisible dirt," said the children.

Life and her friend the frog were too sick and weak to walk, so the children carried them. They followed the water for a long time until they reached the dark force—a huge garbage dump where they found old paint cans, batteries, plastic buckets, bottles, and all sorts of other debris. They realized the garbage was the reason the water in the lake was poisoned.

"We need to get more help so that we can clean and help our nature to feel good again," said Life.

The children ran home to get their parents and friends. They all helped to clean in and around the lake and to make the water fresh and clean again. The leaves returned to the trees, the birds came back and chirped loudly, and the flowers blossomed in all the colors of the rainbow. Life and her friend the frog also became healthy and started to play with the fish in the water. Everything was the way it should be and they lived happily ever after.

Together we are strong. When we take care of ourselves in the best way we can, we also take care of nature and Mother Earth.

Shine like a star, glow like the sun, and feel peace from within. Let your life be a Green Miracle!

Thank you to:

Mother Earth and Father Sky, who are always there giving us green gifts.

My husband Sam and our daughter Saga, your love is a miracle.

My mother, who always believes in what I create, and who is a great example of how Green Smoothies make people shine.

Jinjee and Storm Talifero and their children, because you opened your hearts and showed me the way to raw food: the magical world. I am eternally grateful to you.

Susanne Hovenäs, for encouragement, joy, and your sharp intellect during the process of creating the book with me. You are beautiful inside and out.

Photographer Anna Hult, your charisma and camera skills shine through in every picture. Thank you for understanding the photos that were in my head.

Robert (Bob), Filippa, Malin, and Andrew, for your stories in the biographical portraits. You inspire thousands!

To my aunt, Christel Palmcrantz Garrick, for being just in time.

You, the reader of this book, who allow the green power to sprout within you.